2017

OCT 1 8 2002

VALUE GUIDE TO

Gas Station

MEMORABILIA

B. J. Summers
Wayne Priddy

COLLECTOR BOOKS
A Division Of Schroeder Publishing Co., Inc.

The current values in this book should be used only as a guide. They are not intended to set prices, which vary from one section of the country to another. Auction prices as well as dealer prices vary greatly and are affected by condition as well as demand. Neither the authors nor the publisher assumes responsibility for any losses that might be incurred as a result of consulting this guide.

Searching For A Publisher?

We are always looking for knowledgeable people considered to be experts within their fields. If you feel that there is a real need for a book on your collectible subject and have a large comprehensive collection, contact Collector Books.

On the cover: Texaco Fire Chief sign $80.00; Crown shaped globe $350.00; Shell clam-shaped globe $500.00; Mobilgas globe with Pegasus $600.00; Phillips 66 Shield shaped globe $250.00–350.00; Gulf light-up sign $275.00; Gulf globe $500.00–$750.00; Golden Tip plate $45.00–$80.00; Golden Tip note books $12.00–$22.00; Mendenhall's Guide and Road Map $25.00–$50.00; Gulf Funny Weekly $35.00–$55.00; Shell glass oil bottle $50.00; Standard Oil Cast metal lid $25.00–$35.00; Standard uniform hat $150.00–$200.00; D-X pump glass panel $30.00–$45.00; Premium & Regular pump glass panel $20.00 (for both); Sunoco road map of Michigan $15.00–$18.00; Standard Oil of Indiana automobile lubrication booklet $15.00–$25.00; Milwaukee Tank Works Oil Storage Systems book $55.00–$75.00; Texaco Sky Chief sign $90.00; Marathon uniform hat $75.00–$125.00; Sturdy motor oil 2 gallon tin $25.00; Mobilgas/Socony-vacuum Oil Co. 1945 Ad $10.00; Firestone tire shaped ash tray $10.00–$20.00; brass visible gas pump nozzle $20.00–$55.00; Sinclair road map of Michigan $25.00; Red Crown Gasoline-Ethyl is back pamphlet $8.00–$12.00; Gulf gas gauge ruler $12.00–$15.00. Cloth patches: Marathon $3.50; Cities Service $3.50; Phillips 66 $3.50; Sinclair $3.50; Skelly $3.50; D-X $3.50; Shell $3.50; Shell $3.50; Conoco $3.50; Esso $3.50; Goodrich Tires $3.50.

Cover Design: Beth Summers
Book Design: Sherry Kraus

COLLECTOR BOOKS
P.O. Box 3009
Paducah, Kentucky 42002-3009

B. J. Summers
233 Darnell Road
Benton, KY 42025

Wayne Priddy
P.O. Box 86
Melber, KY 42069

CONTENTS

DEDICATION

Dedications always seem hard for me to do. There are so many people who need to be here. The list could be almost endless. But I certainly can't go without thanking my wife Beth who did all the really hard computer work. Without her help this book would be just another idea wandering around in my head. My mom, Helen Summers, also should be mentioned here for always telling me I could do whatever I set my mind to. Also the folks I mainly deal with at Collector Books, Bill, Billy, Lisa, Gail, Della, and Charley. To all these mentioned above and to all the collectors out there this book is dedicated.

B.J. Summers

This book is dedicated to the late Bob Crawford. Bob was a retired officer of Standard Oil of Kentucky and, until his recent death, one of the most knowledgeable oil historians in the country. Thanks Bob, I wish you could have seen the finished product.

Also I want to remember my dear grandmother, Lela Priddy, and my best friend John. It was

Wilford Priddy (Wayne's father) in back and Wilford's mother, Lela Priddy (Wayne's grandmother), in front of 1926 Star.

a sad day when John, a family friend, stopped by the house to tell of locking the door for the last time on his neighborhood service station. Later John would tell my grandmother that it wasn't the loss of income that was so upsetting, but the fact that friends and customers who stopped by every day now would be a thing of the past. I can now realize that John stopped by my grandmother's because she would understand. Lela Priddy was one of the best mechanics in the business in the early days. People like John and Lela helped make this country what it is today. Working long hours with pay that no one envied, they received much of their rewards in knowing they had done their jobs right. Whether it was fixing a flat tire on a kid's bicycle, or checking out noises under the hood, job satisfaction was important to them. When you pulled in their station for gas and got the tires, oil, water, and windshield serviced, you left with a smile and knew the world was a better place for their being there.

About all we have left now are these memories and a few collectables to help us recall this part of a vanishing America. For all the Johns and Lelas of this country; we hope you know you are not forgotten. This book in large part is dedicated to you.

Wayne W. Priddy

Come with me to those thrilling days of yesteryear when "The Lone Ranger" could be heard galloping from the cloth covered speaker of your radio right into your living room. Or you might tune in just in time to hear all the noises of a too full closet as Fibber McGee opens the door. These were the days before short sleek computerized gas pumps waited for you to get out in the weather and fill your own tank. You knew when you pulled into the corner service station that true service would come to you. Not only would you get gas pumped for you, but the tire pressure, oil, water, and battery levels would get attention. And you could always count on the windows getting cleaned. Or if you wished, while all the work was being done you could go inside and "chew the fat" with the regulars who hung around the station. As a boy in the small community of Lone Oak I knew there was always bubble gum at Mr. Pucketts D-X . When I started driving I knew I could find answers for my ridiculous questions at the corner service station.

Everyone collects for a variety of reasons. But I believe locked into one of the reasons is the need to be surrounded by pleasant memories. There's a certain secure feeling that comes with the soft glow of a lit gas globe in my office. I've heard that people will pay almost any amount to relive a familiar comfortable time. Judging from the steady rise in prices of petroleum items over the past few years this must be true.

Hopefully this book will aid you in the pursuit of pleasing times and memories.

Also the goal of this value guide is to help the beginner and advanced collector alike with prices.

With all this in mind Wayne and I hope you enjoy the book. If it helps with a smile and a bargain it will have been a success.

CREDITS

Collectors Auction Services
Rt 2, Box 431, Oakwood Rd
Oil City, PA 16301
814-677-6070
Mark Anderton
Sherry Mullen

John & Vicki Mahan
1407 N 4th St
Murray, KY 42071

Gene Sonnen
2015 Stanford Ave.
St. Paul, MN 55015

Illinois Antique Center
100 Walnut Street
Peoria, IL 61602
309-673-3354
Kim and Dan Philips

Goodlettsville Antique Mall
213 North Dickerson Pike
Goodlettsville, TN 37072
615-859-7002

Kim and Mary Kokles
P.O. Box 495092
Garland, TX

Larry and Krissy Wingate
Rt. 2 Box 100B I-35 Hwy
Abbott,TX

Ken Black
2003 Red Leaf
Louisville, KY

Don Larson
408 E. 4th
Huxley, IA 50124

Frances Nicholson
West Frankfort, IL 62896

Jerry and Sharron Goulet
G-6345 Fenton Rd
Flint, MI 48507

John Guildford
636 Highland St
Holleston, MA 01746

Nicky Fox
NWS Lake Cherokee
Longview, TX 75603

Rob Vest
430 Greenwood North
DeKalb, IL 60115

Jackie Knott
506 W 13th St
Carrolton, MO 64633

Ken and Karen Coy
Pioneer, OH

John Romagnoli
3640 N. Cornilla
Fresco, CA 93722

Glen Blackmore
1040 Meadow Brook Dr.
Troy, MO 63379

John Hasken
3704 Whitenall Ct.
Louisville, KY

Glen Thompson
3344 Thompson-Schiff Rd
Sidney, OH 45365

John's Custom Fabrication, Inc.
1401 W 97th St
Bloomington, MN 55431

Donald and Barbara Linn
P.O. Box 7174
Moore, OK 73453

Iowa Gas Guys, Des Moines, Iowa
Ron Hoyt
John Chance
John Logsdon

Bob Hull
31680 Mills Rd
Avon, OH 44011

John and Cindy Ogle
R & R Antiques
112 West 2nd St
Grand Island, NE 68801

Teresa and Milford Vice
R.R. # 1
Canton, MO 63435

If we have omitted a name that should have been here please accept our apology and be assured it was an oversite and not intentional.

Pricing is always a tough area. If you had a room full of collectors and dealers the chance of finding two that would agree on a single price for an item would be slim to none. There are several factors that influence the price of an item.

First, as in real estate—LOCATION, LOCATION, LOCATION. In the midwest area where I live, a light-up Gulf sign measuring 26" in diameter by 7" deep in very good shape will go in the $100.00–150 .00 range. On the east coast the same sign would probably run in the $200.00–250.00 range, while on the west coast you could expect the price to start at $250.00 and go up from there. This rule isn't chiseled in granite, but I won't be far off. Does this mean you aren't going to get a good buy in a high price region? Of course not, bargains are to be found everywhere. You've just got be willing to search one out.

Second, who you buy from will have a determining factor on the price. A lot of good bargains can be found in the classified section of your local paper. If you don't see what you are looking for try an ad in the "wanted to buy" section. Yard sales in the past have yielded some good bargains, but be prepared to look through several in your search for the ultimate bargain. My formula is about one good sale for every thirty. So you have to look at a lot of clothes and flower vases before you get a shot at the Holy Grail! Trade papers are a good source to use for finding your collectible, but pricing usually won't be at that bargain point we're all looking for today. I've gotten favorable results with a book called *Wanted To Buy* published by Collector Books. You place your own ad telling the selling public what you want to buy. This ad gives you the latitude to not only advertise for items you want, but also to put in your price guidelines. Swap meets seem to have the luck of not only having the highest prices but also some of the lowest. My experience has shown that if you are willing to take your time and search a meet thoroughly you can usually find some good buys. A couple of good meets held annually are in Iowa and Ohio. Some dealers are willing to discount an item, while others will get upset at the thought of lowering their price. But keep in mind when buying from a dealer—this is their livelihood you're working with. The dealer has to find good collectible items, which is no small feat in today's environment. Then there is the travel and time tied up in this procurement process. The dealer also has to clean the item, research it, do the paperwork on it, let it sit on a shelf until the right buyer comes along, and then pay taxes on the piece. So I try to be understanding when a dealer starts to foam at the mouth when I suggest a lower value than the ticket price. At that time the decision is mine. Do I want the piece badly enough to pay the sticker price? Or do I walk away? This usually depends on the attitudes and atmosphere at the time. I've paid the price to congenial dealers who wouldn't (or couldn't) come down. But, I have also walked away from less than civilized dealers even if the price was close and the sale could have gone either way. Auctions are usually a good place to get decent buys. There are several reputable phone auction firms in the country. One that handles a varied selection of petroleum related items, is Collectors Auction Services in Oil City, Pennsylvania.

Third, timing is important. Around Christmas prices tend to be higher than after the first of the year, for obvious reasons. Timing in the secondary market as far as items that are "hot" will definitely affect the price also. Remember several years back those oil containers were being thrown in the trash without a second thought and now some command prices in the hundreds of dollars.

So a word or two about pricing in this book. Probably we've all looked at price guides and wondered how the author came up with a particular price. In this book you won't have that question. Beside each value in this book you will see a key indicating how a price was determined. A (B) beside the price will indicate an auction bid price. Someone actually paid that price at an auction. Collector prices will be shown by (C), while dealer prices will show a (D). Remember that these dollar amounts are meant to be used only as a guide and the condition of each item very much determines its value.

Year	Patent #	Year	Patent #	Year	Patent #	Year	Patent #	Year	Patent #
		1865	45,685	1895	531,619	1925	1,521,590	1955	2,698,434
1836	1	1866	51,784	1896	552,502	1926	1,568,040	1956	2,728,913
1837	110	1867	60,658	1897	574,369	1927	1,612,700	1957	2,775,762
1838	546	1868	72,959	1898	596,467	1928	1,654,521	1958	2,818,567
1839	1,061	1869	85,503	1899	616,871	1929	1,696,897	1959	2,866,973
1840	1,465	1870	98,460	1900	640,167	1930	1,742,181	1960	2,919,443
1841	1,923	1871	110,617	1901	664,827	1931	1,787,424	1961	2,966,681
1842	2,413	1872	122,304	1902	690,385	1932	1,839,190	1962	3,015,103
1843	2,901	1873	134,504	1903	71 7,521	1933	1,892,663	1963	3,070,801
1844	3,395	1874	146,120	1904	748,567	1934	1,941,449	1964	3,116,487
1845	3,873	1875	158,350	1905	778,834	1935	1,985,878	1965	3,163,865
1846	4,348	1876	171,641	1906	808,618	1936	2,026,516	1966	3,226,729
1847	4,914	1877	185,813	1907	839,799	1937	2,066,309	1967	3,295,143
1848	5,409	1878	198,733	1908	875,679	1938	2,104,004	1968	3,360,800
1849	5,993	1879	211,078	1909	908,436	1939	2,142,080	1969	3,419,907
1850	6,981	1880	223,211	1910	945,010	1940	2,185,170	1970	3,487,470
1851	7,865	1881	236,137	1911	980,178	1941	2,227,418	1971	3,551,909
1852	8,622	1882	251,685	1912	1,013,095	1942	2,268,540	1972	3,631,539
1853	9,512	1883	269,820	1913	1,049,326	1943	2,307,007	1973	3,707,729
1854	10,358	1884	291,016	1914	1,083,267	1944	2,338,081	1974	3,781,914
1855	12,117	1885	310,163	1915	1,123,212	1945	2,366,154	1975	3,858,241
1856	14,009	1886	333,494	1916	1,166,419	1946	2,391,856	1976	3,930,271
1857	16,324	1887	355,291	1917	1,210,389	1947	2,413,675	1977	4,000,520
1858	19,010	1888	375,720	1918	1,251,458	1948	2,433,824	1978	4,065,812
1859	22,477	1889	395,305	1919	1,290,027	1949	2,457,797	1979	4,131,952
1860	26,642	1890	418,665	1920	1,326,899	1950	2,492,944	1980	4,180,867
1861	31,005	1891	443,987	1921	1,364,063	1951	2,536,016	1981	4,242,757
1862	34,045	1892	466,315	1922	1,401,948	1952	2,580,379		
1863	37,266	1893	488,976	1923	1,440,362	1953	2,624,046		
1864	41,047	1894	511,744	1924	1,478,996	1954	2,664,562		

Marathon Multipower Gasoline globe. 15",
3 piece metal band with glass lens globe
$400.00–$500.00.

Let's think about this scenario for a minute. You walk into a supermarket to get some bananas. The banana crop in the produce department is limited. What there is on the produce shelf seems certain to go beyond ripe in a day. So you ask the produce manager if the price can be adjusted for the condition of the merchandise. He then tells you he saw them priced just this morning at another store for that amount. So the price stays. Then the decision is yours. Do you pay what is obviously a price that is too high for the product. Or do you wait until you find produce that is worth the money. Most of us would wait for the good merchandise.

Buying a collectible is that way. A good example of that is in the globe chapter. There we have Marathon Multi Power globe with the runner priced in the $400.00–500.00 range. But this particular globe is cracked. If it were in good condition with no cracks or other problems it would be in the $2,500.00 range. So if you go to someone with this globe and they ask you for $2,500.00 the price is too high. The price must meet the condition of the merchandise. All to often a seller only sees the price of a mint piece and figures all pieces should be priced the same regardless of the condition.

Just remember a value guide is just that—a guide. Most items are in the very good to mint condition. Don't pay more for a piece than it's worth.

Sinclair Gasoline Globe 13½",
1 piece glass globe, $700.00.

Sinclair H-C washed one-piece with fired-on paint.
Be wary of inquery of artist possible not original.
$100.00 (as is condition.)

Those brightly lit gas globes that now adorn dens, offices, restaurants, and the tops of restored pumps began to appear around 1910 to 1915. At first they were all generic and supplied by the pump companies with the purchase of the pump. Early globes were simple in design. The globe makers etched the glass and painted the etchings with such words as "visible gasoline" or simply "gasoline." Other companies just applied fired-on paint to the glass. Other terms such as "correct measure" can be found on these early collectibles.

In the early years there were no standard dimensions for globe holders on the pumps, so some of these globes had four inch and some six inch bases (that is the diameter of the bottom opening of the globe). Six inch bases eventually became the standard except for Standard Oil and a few companies that used a seven inch base. Many of these early globes had metal bands around the base to avoid damaging the glass by the retaining screws as they were tightened while mounting the globe on the pump. At this time most globes were round with flat sides or faces, however some were produced that were actually spherical.

Although these "generic" globes are somewhat rare they don't necessarily bring high prices. This is most likely due to the simplicity of design; they just aren't attractive.

About this same period metal band globes began to be displayed on pumps. A standard metal band or metal frame globe consists of a sheet metal stamping for the band and base, two spring steel snap rings, and two faces or lenses. Again, many early metal bands weren't a standard size or even a standard shape. Some square and rectangular models were used, even a three-sided model was developed. Of the round varieties, dimensions as small as a ten inch diameter face existed. Eventually fifteen inch and sixteen and one-half inch round face bands dominated the market.

Like the one-piece glass, the early metal band globes displayed the generic "gasoline" lettering. However, it didn't take long before petroleum companies began to advertise their products. Quite a variety of media were used as globe faces. Enameled porcelain was used by some companies. Socony Oil produced a beautiful porcelain face, but this forced the use of a spotlight if you wanted your customers to see the globe at night. Oil Creek used a painted punctured tin face, the punctures allowed the interior light to illuminate the brand and the tin provided the durability that was needed around the early gravel highways.

Other companies made use of cast glass faces. Cast glass is very thick, very heavy, and very durable. Companies like Tydol (Tidewater Oil) had their logos cast deep into the glass and then baked on enamel paint with their company colors. This made an impressive, but expensive face. Only a few companies made use of cast faces. It is rare to find one on the antique market today. An even rarer face consists of fired on paint over milk glass. Some faces were produced in leaded stained glass, Texaco probably being the most famous of these.

As stated earlier, two standard sizes of metal bands were settled upon, the fifteen inch and sixteen and one-half inch round bodies with six inch bases. This refers to the size of the face or diameter of the lens the globe holds. The actual globe body diameters still varied, but can be generally divided into two classes. Commonly referred to as "low profile" and "high profile" bodies, they are differentiated by the height or profile of the band when viewing the globe from the side. A low profile globe body is barely visible, allowing the lens to capture all attention. A high profile body has a more rounded band, allowing the color of the band to frame the lens. To draw even more attention to the globe some metal bands were produced with reflectors spaced around the body. These are sometimes referred to by collectors as "diamond" or "jeweled" (see page 60) and they are highly sought after. Standard Oil made use of an even higher, wider profile metal band with a 7" base. In order to ensure the purity of their white band, Pure Oil had the bands porcelainized.

Eventually as petroleum companies realized they could advertise their products on the globes, generic globes gave way to advertising globes. These were still one-piece globes but now they carried the product name and/or logo. Sometimes they carried a side line, such as a tire or battery logo. These early globes weren't always the highest quality. The globe makers were more interested in being prolific rather than producing an heirloom. Some of the earliest one-piece globes had chimneys, similar to but shorter than kerosene lamp chimneys. Apparently some feared the dangerous combination of gas fumes and heat from the globe bulb. Texaco, Gulf, and Standard Oil were among those using the early vented globes. These globes are extremely rare and appear to have been produced with etched logos. Other one-piece globes appeared with painted raised letters or simply fired- on painted logos. The most commonly found of these raised letter globes today is the Gulf globe. Gulf No-Nox was also produced in the raised letter globe. Along with these, Gulf also made extensive use of fired-on logos on one-piece globes.

An important point to remember when buying an early globe is the paint condition. As a general rule collectors seem to agree that paint condition on a raised letter or etched globe is less important. However, on simple fired-on globes, paint condition is everything. Any touch-up or re-painting will affect the price of a globe. As an example: a one-piece Sinclair with fired-on paint in poor condition will run around $350.00, while in mint condition it would probably be in the $1,200.00 to $1,500.00 range.

As the industry evolved so did the artwork on globes. Awesome is the only way to describe a Michigan-Musgo globe picturing an American Indian Chief in full headdress. And some of the one-piece globes began to take on new shapes, changing from the globular and disc shapes to such beauties as the crown for Standard Oil. Shell Oil developed a large clam-shaped globe, Cities Service used a clover-shaped globe and White Eagle gasoline produced a 20" tall, full-feathered, milk glass eagle globe to perch atop their pumps. Other variations include Fleetwing Oil, a company that used a two-piece globe held together by a metal clamp inside the body. While white was by far the dominant color, there was some use of colored glass. Two-piece glass bodies and colored glass globes are extremely rare.

Around the late 1920s, globes with a glass body and two detachable lenses, or three-piece globes, entered the market. Since each company had its own idea as to the size of the lenses and how to attach them, there are many variations on this three-piece globe. The Gill Glass Company of Pennsylvania produced a glass band or body similar to a metal band. The faces attached to this glass body by use of a thin metal retaining ring that surrounded the outside edge of the face and a glass bead on the body. An adjusting screw at the base of the band secured the face. Gill produced many sizes of globe bodies, mostly in the thirteen and one half inch to fourteen inch range. Some companies used a fifteen inch glass body. These bodies used a retaining ring and had a solid flat face. Because they used a flat low profile band they don't appear to be much larger than the thirteen and one half inch bodies. Unfortunately the glass on these fifteen inch models is extremely thin and great care should be used in their handling. Gill also produced what collectors call a ripple body globe. These were made of clear ripple-textured glass. Different colors of paint were then fired onto the inside of the globe producing a beautiful band when illuminated. These were available in clear, white, red, green, blue, orange, tan, yellow and possibly a few other colors. Over the years many of these globes have been repainted, altering the original color. But, repainted or not, these are highly desirable globes with values reaching $1,000.00 or more.

The most common three-piece glass globes were made by CAPCO (Cincinnati Advertising Products Company). These were made in wide and narrow body thirteen and one-half inch models and in a wide-body twelve and one-half inch model. These bodies have solid sides equipped with two small holes to allow passage of machine screws for attaching the faces. The glass was thick and when the faces are added the globes are fairly heavy. The twelve and one-half inch models were used extensively by Gulf Oil and American Oil. The plastic band globe was patented in the 1930s, but they didn't come into wide acceptance until the late 1940s and 50s. These were produced in the standard white and a variety of other colors. CAPCO also produced an oval-shaped body, which, as far as we know, was made only in white. Plastic narrow-body globes were the most prevalent, making the wide-body plastic globe more sought after. Phillips 66 favored the wide-body style and also made use of a shield-shaped plastic body with shield-shaped plastic lenses.

Plastic body globe faces may be distinguished from glass body globe faces by the thickness of the glass lens and the depth of the notches for attachment. Plastic body faces use thin glass and shallow notches. While you might think a plastic body globe would be less expensive, this isn't always the case.

Plastic body globes with many colors (especially 5 or more) and picture globes bring very high prices. By the 1960s and 1970s the gas globe seemed to have gone the way of the full-service gas station, with only a few companies holding onto the globe tradition. Vandalism and changing economic dynamics within oil companies have played a large part in the demise of these advertising icons.

Aetna Motor Gasoline, red and white lens
(Mount Aetna in the background)
Aetna Oil Company
Louisville, Kentucky
Aetna was bought by Ashland in 1950.
13½", 3 piece, all glass globe
$375.00–$475.00 (C)

Allfire with red anchor in center
The Security Oil Company
Wichita, Kansas
13½", 3 piece, red ripple glass band glass lens globe
$1,950.00–$2,250.00(C)

Amoco red, white and blue lens
American Oil Company
Troy, New York
1½", 3 piece, glass globe
Amoco brand is seen mostly on 12½" globes
$325.00 (B)

Ashland flying octanes lenses
Unusual Ashland lens on clear glass beside usual white face
Ashland Oil Company, Ashland, Kentucky
$55.00–$80.00 each lens (C)

Ashland (speed letters)
flying octanes red, white and blue lens
Ashland Oil Company
Ashland, Kentucky
13½", 3 piece, plastic globe
$275.00–$325.00 (C)

Ashland (speed letters) flying octanes red,
white and blue lens
Ashland Oil Company
Ashland, Kentucky
13½", glass lens only
$225.00 (B)

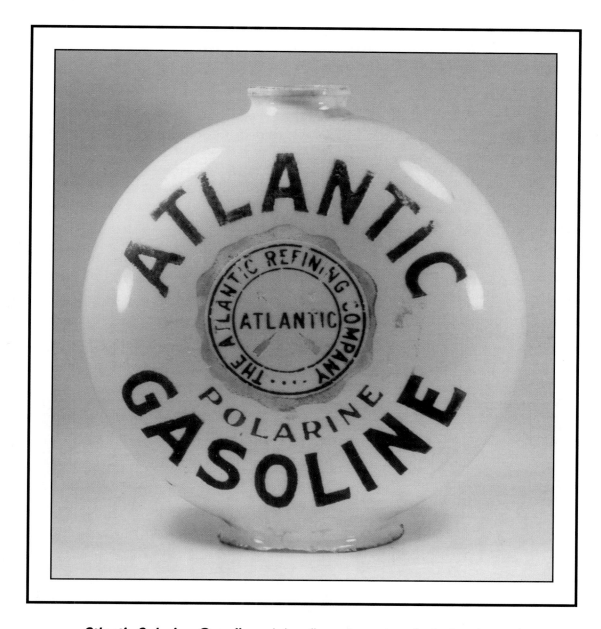

Atlantic Polarine Gasoline globe (logo in center, faded red paint)
Atlantic Refining Company, Philadelphia, Pennsylvania
15", one-piece glass chimney top globe. Top metal vent missing.
Chimney top globes are very rare. Gas companies were wary of the
combustible combination of the heat from these globes and the gas fumes,
so they used this chimney style for a short period of time.
Circa 1915–1920
$2,000.00–2,200.00 (C)

Atlantic Gasoline (logo in center) lens
Atlantic Refining Company
Philadelphia, Pennsylvania
16½", metal band globe with glass lens
$550.00 (D)

Atlantic Hi-Arc
Atlantic Refining Company
Philadelphia, Pennsylvania
16½", metal band globe
with glass lens
$375.00 (B)

Atlantic White Flash
Atlantic Refining Company
Philadelphia, Pennsylvania
16½", metal band globe
with glass lens
$650.00 (B)

BARECO Super-Gas with Ethyl Logo
Barnsdall Refining Company
Barnsdall, Oklahoma
13½", 3 piece, plastic band globe with glass lens
$275.00–$350.00 (C)

Bell Regular (bell in center) lens
Bell Oil and Gas Company
Grandfield and Tulsa, Oklahoma
13½", 3 piece glass,
white glass ripple band globe
with metal base and glass lens
$1,600.00 (C)

Bell (bell & oil derrick in center bottom) lens
Bell Oil Company
Grandfield and Tulsa, Oklahoma
13½", 3 piece glass, orange glass ripple band
globe with metal base and glass lens
Bell Oil Company used variations of this logo from
the 1930s to the early 1960s.
$1,900.00 (C)

Courtesy of Gene Sonnen

Browder Ethyl Gasoline (Ethyl logo with Ethyl Corporation at bottom) globe
13½", 3 piece, plastic band glass lens globe
$300.00 (B)

Campeco Aviation Gasoline
Campeco Oil Company
15", 1 piece, glass globe (rare)
$900.00 (C)

Courtesy of Ken Black

Champion Gasoline
with #1 race car art in center
circa 1920s
15", lens for metal band
$950.00–$1,100.00 (C)
(price is for pair)

Champion Ethyl lens
Champion Refining Company
Ohio
13½", 3 piece, glass globe with glass lens
$275.00–$325.00 (C)

Champlin Gasoline with Ethyl logo in center lens
Champlin Oil Company
Enid, Oklahoma
13½", 3 piece, glass band globe with glass lens
$425.00 (B)

Champlin Presto Gasoline lens
Champlin Oil Company
Enid, Oklahoma
13½", 3 piece glass band globe with glass lens
$335.00 (B)

Champlin Gasoline, use Champlin Oils in center lens
Champlin Oil Company
Enid, Oklahoma
13½", 3 piece, glass band globe with glass lens
$375.00–$425.00(C)

Cities Service Koolmotor clover leaf shape lens
Cities Service Oil Company
Tulsa, Oklahoma
15" tall, 3 piece, glass globe
Cities Service Oil Company was the only company
to use this clover shape.
$925.00 (D)

Cities Service Oils, Once—Always
(clover leaf logo in center)
Cities Service Oil Company
Tulsa, Oklahoma
15", metal band with glass globe
circa 1920s–1930s
$350.00–$550.00 (C)

Cities Service (clover leaf logo at top)
clover leaf shape lens
Cities Service Oil Company
Tulsa, Oklahoma
3 piece, glass globe
circa 1930s–1940s
$450.00(B)

Cities Service (name within clover leaf logo)
Cities Service Oil Company, Tulsa, Oklahoma
13½", 3 piece, plastic band with glass lens globe
circa 1950s
$200.00–$300.00 (C)

Clark *globe*
Clark Oil Company
St. Louis, Missouri
(Clark was one of the last oil companies to use globes, finally removing them in the early 1980s)
13½", 3 piece glass band with glass lens globe
$250.00–$350.00 (C)

This photograph is of B.J.'s dad, Tom Summers, in the early 1940s in St. Louis, Missouri. It was taken just a short time before he joined the Navy after the attack on Pearl Harbor. Notice the Clark Oil signs and products in the background.

Courtesy of Gene Sonnen

Coastal Anti-Knock picture globe
(art of sea gulls at center)
13½", 3 piece, glass band glass lens
globe with screw-on base
$800.00–$900.00 (C)

Conoco Gasoline with logo (REG U. S. PAT. OFF)
in center lens
Continental Oil Company
Denver, Colorado
13½", 3 piece, plastic band globe with glass lens
manufactured in USA at bottom
$250.00 (B)

Conoco Gasoline with Ethyl logo in center lens
Continental Oil Company
Denver, Colorado
(this appears to be early glass faces in newer
plastic bands. If it is, the price range should be
$200.00–$250.00)
13½", 3 piece globe
$375.00 (B)

CO–OP globe (white band, red lens with white and black trim)
Farmers Industries
Farm Co-operatives
Kansas City, Missouri
13½", 3 piece, glass wide band globe with glass lens
$300.00–$350.00 (C)

CO–OP Globe (white with green letters)
Farmers Industries
Farm Co-operatives
Kansas City, Missouri
13½", Gill band globe with metal screw-on base
$350.00–$450.00 (C)

Use **CO-OP** Globe (with Ethyl Logo)
Farmers Industries
Farm Co-operatives
Kansas City, Missouri
13½", Gill band globe with glass lens
$375.00–$450.00 (C)

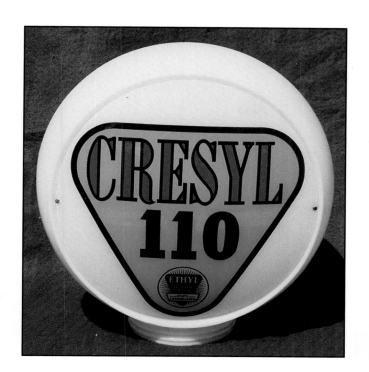

Cresyl 110 with Ethyl trademark at bottom
of globe
Site Oil Company
Clayton, Missouri
13½", 3 piece, glass band with screw-on base
(missing on this one) and glass lens globe
circa 1940s
$325.00–$375.00 (C)

Crown Standard KY Gasoline
Standard Oil of Kentucky
Louisville, Kentucky
16½", metal band with glass lens globe
circa 1920s
$600.00 (C)

Crown Extra (red & white)
Standard Oil of Kentucky
Louisville, Kentucky
13½", plastic band with glass lens globe
circa 1950s
$175.00–$225.00 (C)

Super Crown Extra (green & white)
Standard Oil of Kentucky
Louisville, Kentucky
13½", 3 piece, plastic band with glass lens globe
circa 1950s
$150.00–$200.00 (C)

Crown (red & white)
Standard Oil of Kentucky
Louisville, Kentucky
13½", 3 piece, glass band with glass lens globe
circa 1940s
$225.00–$275.00 (C)

Cushing Anti-Knock (logo in center)
Cushing Refining and Gasoline Company
Cushing, Oklahoma
13½", 3 piece, glass band with glass lens globe
$400.00 (B)

Cushing *(Ethyl logo in lower center)*
Cushing Refining and Gasoline Company
Cushing, Oklahoma
13½", 3 piece, glass band with glass lens globe
$375.00–$425.00 (C)

Deep Rock Super Gasoline
13½", 3 piece plastic band with glass lens globe
$175.00–$225.00 (C)

Deep Rock Gasoline
with older Ethyl Logo at center
13½", plastic band with glass lens globe
$225.00 (D)

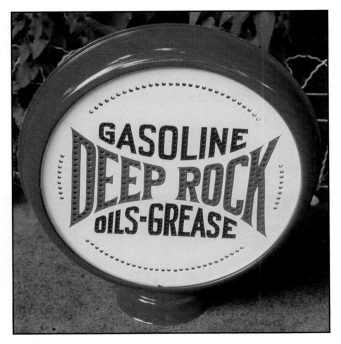

Courtesy of Gene Sonnen

Deep Rock Gasoline/Oils/Grease globe
15½", 3 piece, metal band
with perforated face globe (rare)
circa 1915–1925
$950.00–$1,250.00 (C)

Diamond (diamond shape with lettering within)
Mid Continent Petroleum
Tulsa, Oklahoma
(The Diamond Logo was used in the 1920s and 1930s
and was later to become D-X.)
15", 1 piece glass globe, $775.00–$900.00 (C)

Diamond NevrNox Gasolene Product
Mid Continent Petroleum
Tulsa, Oklahoma
15", 1 piece glass globe
$1,575.00 (B)

Power with diamond shape
Mid Continent Petroleum
Tulsa, Oklahoma
13¾", wide band 3 piece, glass band globe
(the globe has an external band around the
lens to hold it in place.)
$300.00–$400.00 (C)

Power with diamond shape and "G"
Mid Continent Petroleum
Tulsa, Oklahoma
13¾", 3 piece, glass band globe
(the globe has an external band around
the lens to hold it in place.)
$375.00 (D)

D-X Ethyl Lubricating Motor Fuel with diamond shape art
Mid Continent Petroleum
Tulsa, Oklahoma
(The Diamond logo was used in the 1920s and 1930s
and was later to become D-X.)
13½", 3 piece, glass band with glass lens globe
$500.00 (D)

D-X Boron with rocket attachment
Mid Continent Petroleum
Tulsa, Oklahoma
13½", 3 piece, plastic band with glass
lens globe
circa mid 1950s
$350.00 (C)

D-X Boron diamond shape logo
Mid Continent Petroleum
Tulsa, Oklahoma
13½", 3 piece, plastic band glass lens globe
$175.00–$225.00 (C)

D-X Lubricating Gasoline diamond shape logo
Mid Continent Petroleum
Tulsa, Oklahoma
13½", 3 piece, plastic band glass lens globe
$225.00 (C)

Diamond D-X Lubricating Motor Fuel
diamond shape logo
Mid Continent Petroleum
Tulsa, Oklahoma
13½", 3 piece, glass wide band glass lens globe
$350.00–$475.00 (C)

Dixie *with two crossed rebel flags and*
confederate cap
13½", 3 piece, plastic band glass lens globe
This appears to be a "Fantasy" globe. It
combines elements of a Dixie & Rebel globe.
$175.00–$225.00 (C)

Dixie Ethyl *with Ethyl logo*
Distributors, Inc.
Ann Arbor, Michigan
13½", 3 piece, yellow plastic band glass
lens globe
$275.00–$375.00 (C)

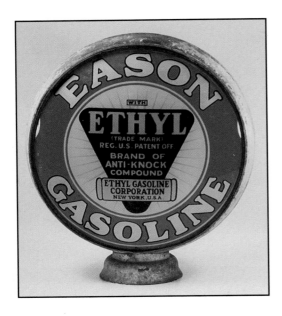

Eason Gasoline
with Ethyl trademark in center
Eason Oil Company
Oklahoma
15", 3 piece, metal band glass lens globe
$425.00–$550.00 (C)

Esso Script
Standard Oil Company
New Jersey
15", 3 piece, metal band glass lens globe
The Standard Oil Co. of New Jersey (Esso)
used this script logo from the early 1920's
to the early 1930's. Standard also used
bold type lettering on globes but the script
is more desirable and more valuable.
$500.00 (B)

Essolene *globe*
Standard Oil of New Jersey, NY, NY
low profile 16½" metal band glass lens globe
$450.00–$550.00 (C)

Extron globe
Standard Oil of Ohio
Cleveland, Ohio
13½", 3 piece, glass band glass lens globe
$225.00–$275.00 (C)

Farmer's Union with Ethyl Logo globe
Farmer's Union Central Exchange
St. Paul, Minnesota
13½", plastic band glass lens globe
(originally had a glass band.)
$225.00–$350.00 (C)

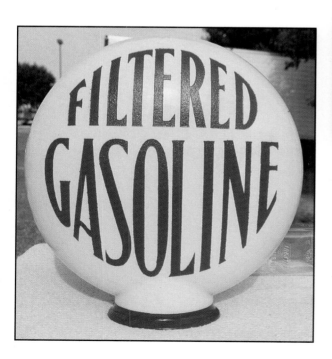

Filtered Gasoline
Generic globe
early one piece glass globe
$500.00–$750.00 (C)

Fleet-Wing *with art of flying bird*
Spears & Riddle Company
Wheeling, West Virginia
(bought out by SOHIO)
13½", 3 piece, glass band with glass lens globe
$275.00–$325.00 (C)

Flying A Gasoline *(A with wings logo)*
Associated Oil Company
San Francisco, California
13½", 3 piece, gill band with glass lens globe
$375.00–$450.00 (C)

Ford Benzol *globe*
Ford Motor Company
Dearborn, Michigan
sold by a few Detroit Michigan Ford dealers
One piece glass globe
$2,500.00–$4,000.00 (C)

Courtesy of Gene Sonnen

Gasolene globe (red lettering)
One piece etched globe
$700.00–$800.00 (C)

Gaylor gasoline globe
13½", 3 piece, piece glass band with
glass lens globe
$325.00–$425.00 (C)

Courtesy of Gene Sonnen

Genoco globe
15" 3 piece, metal band with glass lens globe
$450.00–$550.00 (C)

Globe Gasoline *with globe of earth at*
North and South American Continents
Globe Oil Company, McPherson, Kansas
13½", 3 piece, metal band glass lens globe
$900.00–$1,000.00 (C)

Gladiator Gasoline U. S. Motor Specifications *globe*
(with crossed swords at top)
13½", 3 piece, glass globe
$325.00–$450.00 (C)

That Good Gulf Gasoline *globe*
Gulf Oil Company
Pittsburgh, Pennsylvania
One piece glass raised letter globe
$900.00–$1,100.00 (C)

No-Nox Gulf Motor Fuel *globe*
Gulf Oil Company
Pittsburgh, Pennsylvania
One piece glass raised letter globe
$1,000.00–$1,300.00 (C)

The man in this photograph is B.J.'s grandfather, Ted Harper. At the time this photograph was taken (between 1925 and 1932) he was truck supervisor for Gulf Oil in Paducah. His job at the time consisted of keeping the gas delivery trucks manned and on schedule. In addition he was responsible for sales of Gulf products in his territory. B.J.'s uncle Mac (Ted's son) when he was a small boy would occasionally go on the truck routes with Ted. Mac said the trips were usually over rough, rutted, bumpy roads to small country stores. At the end of the arduous trip sometimes only 50 or 60 gallons of gas might be needed by the store owner. The gas was transferred by hand from the truck to the storage tank in buckets. Products such as oils and greases were kept on a ledge on the side of the truck. Mack was just barely tall enough to reach a gallon oil can and slip it off the edge to get it down, but he couldn't get one loaded back up on the shelf. After working for Gulf in this position, B.J.'s grandad then went to work for Shell Oil Company.

Gulf globe
Gulf Oil Company
Pittsburgh, Pennsylvania
One piece glass with metal screw-on base
raised letter globe
$500.00–$750.00 (C)

Haney's Gasoline Independent Dependable
(H with arrow through center)
Haney Oil Company
15", 3 piece, metal band glass lens globe
$650.00 (B)

Hudson Regular Hi-Octane Gas *(with art of gas tanker truck in center) globe*
Hudson Oil Company
Kansas City, Kansas
13½", plastic band glass lens globe
$450.00 (C)

Courtesy of Gene Sonnen

Husky *picture globe (with art of Husky dog)*
13½", 3 piece, glass gill band with glass lens globe
$3,000.00 (C)

Indian Gas *(Red Dot at center)*
Indian Refining Company
New York, New York
Indian Oil Company was purchased by Texaco in 1931. Texaco sold Indian as their low-priced third grade gas until the early 1940s.
13½", 3 piece, glass band glass lens globe
$400.00 (B)

Imperial Refineries
(yellow and red shield in center)
Imperial Refineries
Clayton, Missouri
13½", 3 piece, plastic band glass lens globe
$150.00–$225.00 (C)

Rare 1965 **Imperial Refineries**
50th Anniversary Globe
Imperial Refineries
Clayton, Missouri
13½", 3 piece, glass band glass lens globe
$675.00 (C)

Courtesy of Gene Sonnen

Imperial Gasoline & Oils
Boner Oil Company
12", 3 piece, metal band with glass lens globe
(Only one known to exist)
$1,000.00 (C)

Kanotex Bondified *globe*
Arkansas City, Kansas
13½", orange ripple glass band glass lens,
screw-on base globe
$1,200.00–$1,400.00 (C)

Kanotex *(Ethyl trademark in center)*
Arkansas City, Kansas
13½", 3 piece, ripple band with metal
base glass lens globe
$1,200.00 (B)

Keystone *(Ethyl trademark at center bottom) globe*
Elk Refining Company
Charleston, West Virginia
13½", gill band with copper screw-on
base glass lens globe
$400.00 (C)

High-test, Anti-knock Koolmotor Gasolene lens
Cities Service Oil Company
Tulsa, Oklahoma
15", metal band glass lens globe
$950.00–$1,400.00 (C)

High-test Koolmotor Anti-knock globe
Cities Service Oil Company
Tulsa, Oklahoma
15", 3 piece, metal band glass lens globe
$500.00 (B)

Courtesy of Gene Sonnen

Kunz Gasoline picture globe
(art of pine trees and early automobile)
Kunz Oil Company
3 piece, metal band with glass lens globe
(Only one known to exist)
$3,800.00–$4,400.00 (C)

Lion globe (featuring lion artwork at top)
Lion Oil Company
El Dorado, Arkansas
13½", glass band glass lens globe
$450.00–$600.00 (C)

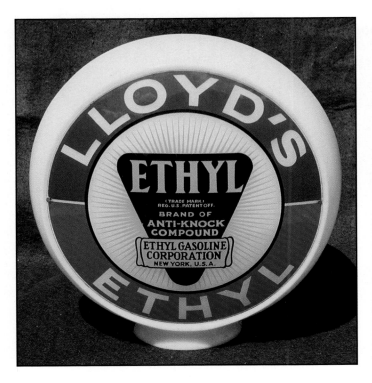

Leonard globe
Leonard Refineries
Alma, Michigan
13½", 3 piece, plastic band glass lens globe
$150.00–$200.00 (C)

Lloyd's (Ethyl trademark in center)
13½", 3 piece, glass band glass lens globe
$350.00–$450.00 (C)

Magnolia Gasoline *globe*
Magnolia Petroleum Company
Dallas, Texas
16½", low profile metal band with glass lens globe
circa 1920s
$1,600.00–$2,150.00 (C)

Magnolia Anti-Knock Gasoline *globe*
Magnolia Petroleum Company
Dallas, Texas
16½", 3 piece, metal band with glass lens globe
(fairly rare)
circa 1920s
$1,600.00–$2,150.00 (C)

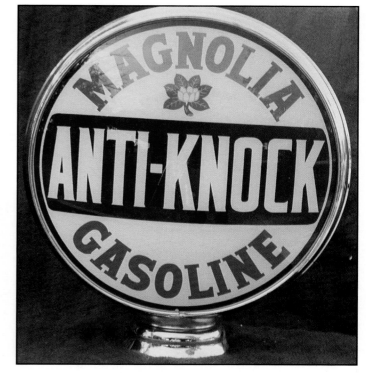

Malco *globe*
Malco Refining Company
Roswell, New Mexico
13½", 3 piece, plastic band with glass lens globe
circa 1950s
$285.00 (C)

Marathon Multipower Gasoline (with runner) globe
Transcontinental Oil Company
New York, New York
15", 3 piece, metal band with glass lens
globe (cracked)
(If perfect this globe would command $2,500.00.)
$400.00–$500.00 (C)

Marine Gasoline globe (featuring seahorse art)
Marine Oil Company
St. Louis, Missouri
13½", 3 piece, plastic band
with glass lens globe (dark blue)
circa 1950s
$225.00–$325.00 (C)

Marine Gasoline globe (featuring seahorse art)
Marine Oil Company
St. Louis, Missouri
13½", 3 piece, plastic band
with glass lens globe (aqua blue)
The aqua color is a common color for the 1940s
glass bodied globes.
$275.00–$375.00 (C)

Me-tee-or A Higher Test Gasoline *globe*
W. H. Barber & Company
Chicago, Illinois
15", 3 piece, metal band with glass lens globe
(This company was bought by Pure Oil
Company in 1945.)
$550.00–$750.00 (C)

Mobilgas *lens with Pegasus*
Socony Vacuum
16½", lens only
$75.00 (C)

Mobilgas Aircraft *with Pegasus*
Socony Vacuum
15", 3 piece, metal band glass lens globe
$950.00 (C)

Mobilgas *with Pegasus at top*
Socony Vacuum
16½", 3 piece, metal band glass lens globe
$450.00–$600.00 (C)

Mobilgas Ethyl *with Pegasus at top*
Socony Vacuum
16½", 3 piece, metal band glass lens globe
$475.00–$625.00 (C)

Mobile Premium *with Pegasus at top center*
Socony Vacuum
13½", 3 piece, plastic band glass lens globe
$150.00–$225.00 (C)

Mobilfuel Diesel *globe*
Socony Vacuum
New York, New York
13½", 3 piece, glass band glass lens globe
$275.00–$375.00 (C)

Hi-Neighbor, Mo-Jo, X-Tane Premium
14", 3 piece, glass globe
$225.00–$275.00 (C)

MonaMotor Gasoline *globe*
Monarch Manufacturing Company
Council Bluffs, Iowa
1 piece glass globe with baked-on paint
(fairly rare)
circa 1920s
$1,200.00–$1,675.00 (C)

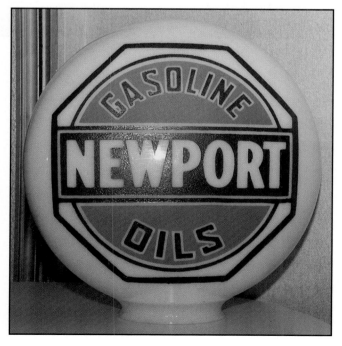

Newport Gasoline/Oils *globe*
1 piece glass globe (rare)
$1,150.00–$1,700.00 (C)

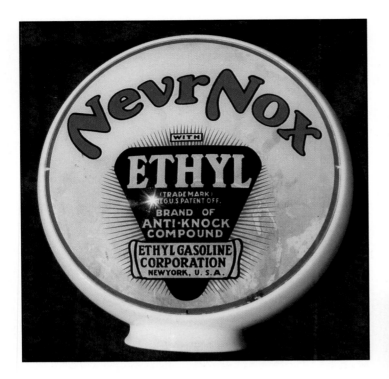

NevrNox with Ethyl logo globe
Mid Continent Petroleum Company
Tulsa, Oklahoma
13½", 3 piece, glass band with glass lens globe
$325.00–$425.00 (C)

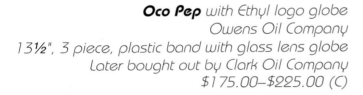

Oco Pep with Ethyl logo globe
Owens Oil Company
13½", 3 piece, plastic band with glass lens globe
Later bought out by Clark Oil Company
$175.00–$225.00 (C)

Just Fine Gasoline Oil Creek globe
Oil Creek Refining Company
Oil City, Pennsylvania
metal band with metal perforated painted faces globe
circa 1915
$850.00–$1,000.00 (C)

Courtesy of Gene Sonnen

Oil Creek Ethyl *picture globe (art of oil derricks and mountains)*
Oil Creek Refining Company
Oil City, Pennsylvania
3 piece, metal band with glass lens globe
$1,250.00–$1,600.00 (C)

Onyx Petroleum Products *globe*
Texas
15", 3 piece, metal band with glass lens globe
circa 1920s–1930s
$400.00–$500.00 (C)

Paige Sales Service *globe*
one piece glass globe (very rare)
$1,700.00–$2,100.00 (C)

Courtesy of Jackie Knott

Pankey globe
Pankey Oil Company
Brookfield, Missouri
spherical glass globe only 2 known to exist
circa 1915
$1,800.00 (C)

Paraland globe
marketed by Phillips 66
Bartlesville, Oklahoma
3 piece, oval plastic band glass lens globe
$225.00 (D)

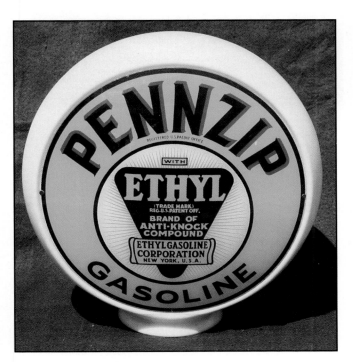

Pennzip Gasoline with Ethyl logo globe
Pennzoil Company
13½", 3 piece, glass band with glass lens globe
$375.00–$475.00 (C)

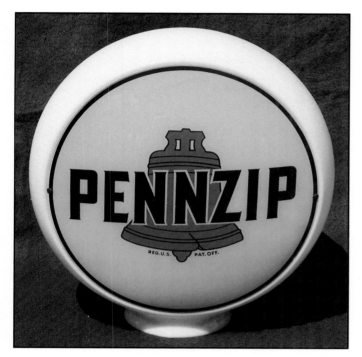

Pennzip globe with bell
Pennzoil Company
13½", 3 piece, glass band with glass lens globe
$400.00–$500.00 (C)

Phillips Unique
Phillips Petroleum Company
Bartlesville, Oklahoma
13½", 3 piece, glass band with glass lens globe
(this was Phillips third grade in gasoline)
$550.00–$650.00 (C)

Phillips 66 (with shield) Ethyl globe
Phillips Petroleum Company
Bartlesville, Oklahoma
13½", 3 piece, plastic band glass lens globe
$400.00 (B)

Phillips 66 (with shield)
Phillips Petroleum Company
Bartlesville, Oklahoma
13½", 3 piece, plastic band glass lens globe
$250.00–$400.00 (C)

Phillips 66 (with shield) **Flite-Fuel**
Phillips Petroleum Company
Bartlesville, Oklahoma
13½", 3 piece, plastic band glass lens globe
$285.00 (D)

Phillips 66 (shield-shaped) **Flite-Fuel**
Phillips Petroleum Company
Bartlesville, Oklahoma
3 piece, plastic band plastic lens
shield-shaped globe
$250.00–$350.00 (C)

Power Flash Independent Gasoline picture globe (featuring spark plug and flash art)
fantastically restored jeweled metal band glass lens globe
$4,000.00–$5,000.00 (C)

Both photos on this page are courtesy of Gene Sonnen

Compare this unrestored band to the Power Flash band that has been restored. These are very rare and very hard to find.
$1,600.00–$2,200.00 (C)

Powerine globe
Powerine Oil Company
Denver, Colorado
15", 3 piece, metal band with glass lens globe
circa 1920s–1930s
$350.00–$450.00 (C)

Premium Ethyl globe
13½", 3 piece, white ripple glass band
with glass lens globe
$1,000.00–$1,300.00 (C)

Purol Pep globe
The Pure Oil Company
Chicago, Illinois
15", 3 piece, metal band glass lens globe
$400.00 (B)

PURE globe
The Pure Oil Company
Chicago, Illinois
15", 3 piece, metal band glass lens globe
$400.00 (B)

Woco Pep Trade Mark, King of Motor Fuel
Wufford Oil Company
Atlanta, Georgia
This company merged with Pure Oil in the 1920s
15", 3 piece, metal band glass lens globe
This metal band is white porcelain, adding
significantly to the value of the globe
$500.00–$750.00 (C)

Red Crown Gasoline with crown in center
Standard Oil of Indiana
Chicago, Illinois
16½", 3 piece, metal band glass lens globe
circa 1920s
$750.00 (B)

Red Crown Gasoline *with crown in center*
3 piece, metal band glass lens globe
circa 1920s
$600.00–$1,000.00 (C)

Red Head Hi-Octane Gasoline
globe with boy in center
Red Head Oil Company
Wooster, Ohio
13½", 3 piece, glass band glass lens globe
(Only one known to exist.)
$3,500.00–$4,500.00 (C)

Red Hat Motor Oil/Gasoline *globe*
with trademark tophat in center
Independent Oil Member of America
Chicago, Illinois
15", 3 piece, metal band glass lens globe
$1,900.00–$2,400.00 (C)

Refiners Pioneer Distributors *with* ***Ethyl Trademark***
Refiners Oil Company
Dayton, Ohio
General Motors discovered that lead added to gaso-line improved performance and began marketing Ethyl through Refiners Oil Company during the 1920s.
16½", 3, piece, metal band glass lens globe
$550.00 (C)

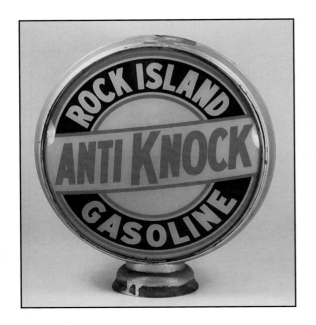

Rock Island Anti Knock Gasoline
Rock Island Refining Company
Indianapolis, Indiana
15", 3 piece, metal band glass lens globe
$450.00–$500.00 (C)

Saturn Regular
3 piece, oval plastic band glass lens globe
$225.00–$275.00 (C)

Save with Savex Gasoline
Milton Oil Company
Sedalia, Missouri
13½", 3 piece, glass band glass lens globe
$325.00–$375.00 (C)

Shell *clam shaped globe*
Shell Oil Company
1 piece clam shaped glass globe
$500.00 (B)

"Sizzling Lizards...HOT!"

Take the machines and materials of our temperate civilization into 120° of desert heat and you get some new problems . . .

Actually, 100 octane Aviation Gasoline—volatile, temperamental—stewing in a fuel dump of steel drums, begins to separate into its constituent parts . . . gets "gummy."

This was one of the hazards of a war in which aviation gasoline must be kept "on tap" in the hottest spots of all geography.

* * *

SCIENTISTS AT THE "UNIVERSITY OF PETROLEUM," Shell's research laboratories—who made possible the first commercial production of 100 octane fuel back in 1934—had a special interest in solving this new war-

time problem. The answer was a long time coming, but they have it now—a new, revolutionary "inhibitor."

It's a "stopper"—a "preventer"—it "inhibits" the separation of aviation fuel. A few drops in a barrel of fuel, and its molecules stay put. Gum doesn't form . . .

STORAGE OF 7 YEARS, AT 120°, IS POSSIBLE. Although it is not yet in production, the Army Air Forces have accepted Shell's new inhibitor as a research achievement of prime importance to desert operations.

Solution of this war problem was the immediate goal. But you will notice that practically every advance of Shell Research has a continuing value. In the future world of

air travel and transport, for example, an "inhibitor" for aviation fuel stored in the desert will contribute to the safety and smooth operation of the air fleets.

First oil refinery to win the Army-Navy "E"— Shell's Wood River Refinery

SHELL RESEARCH
Sword of Today
Plowshare of Tomorrow

Shell Gasoline *with art of clamshell*
Shell Oil Company
jeweled band glass lens globe
$11,775.00 (B)
($9,775.00 for the lens and $2,000 for jeweled band.)
Lenses and band combined, this may be the highest price ever paid for a single globe.

Sinclair Dino Gasoline
globe with dinosaur at top
Sinclair Refining Company
Chicago, Illinois
13½", 3 piece, plastic band with glass lens globe
$175.00–$225.00 (C)

Sinclair Gasoline globe
(blue-green letters)
Sinclair Refining Company
Chicago, Illinois
One piece spherical glass globe
$1,750.00 (C)

Sinclair Gasoline globe
(red letters)
Sinclair Refining Company
Chicago, Illinois
One piece spherical glass globe
$1,750.00 (C)

Sinclair Dino Supreme with dinosaur logo at top
Sinclair Refining Company, Chicago, Illinois
13½", 3 piece, plastic band glass lens globe
The brontosaurus was registered in 1932 as Sinclair's logo. Sinclair presented a dinosaur exhibit
at the 1933 World's Fair in Chicago. In 1935 their ad campaign was a dinosaur stamp book with a
different dinosaur issued each week. In 1964 nine life size Dinos were floated on the Hudson River
to the site of the New York World's Fair. A souvenir of that World's Fair was a wax model Dino.
Dino is still in use in the Rocky Mountains and Plains States.
$250.00 (D)

Sinclair Gasoline
Sinclair Refining Company
Chicago, Illinois
1 piece glass globe
$700.00–$900.00 (C)

Sinclair H-C Gasoline
Sinclair Refining Company
Chicago, Illinois
13½", 3 piece, glass band glass lens globe
$300.00–$400.00 (C)

Sinclair Power-X over 100 Octane *globe*
Sinclair Oil Company
New York, New York
13½", 3 piece, plastic band with glass lens globe
circa 1950s
$175.00–$250.00 (C)

Sinclair H-C Gasoline *globe*
Sinclair Oil Company
New York, New York
13½", 3 piece, plastic band with glass lens globe
circa 1950s
$150.00–$225.00 (C)

Skelly Premium
Skelly Oil Company
Tulsa, Oklahoma
13½", 3 piece, glass wide band glass lens globe
$250.00–$300.00 (C)

Skelly globe
Skelly Oil Company
Tulsa, Oklahoma
One piece glass globe with baked-on paint
This globe was made in regular or inverted
style which was designed to be mounted
under the canopy or roof of a gas station.
$400.00–$600.00 (C)

Fortified Skelly Gasoline globe
Skelly Oil Company, Tulsa, Oklahoma
13½", 3 piece, glass band with glass lens globe
circa 1940s
$275.00 (B)

Skelly Aromax with Ethyl Trademark
Skelly Oil Company
Tulsa, Oklahoma
13½", 3 piece, glass band
with metal base glass lens globe
$425.00 (B)

Skelly Powermax
Skelly Oil Company
Tulsa, Oklahoma
13½", 3 piece, plastic band glass lens globe
$175.00–$250.00 (C)

Skelly Aromax
Skelly Oil Company
Tulsa, Oklahoma
13½", 3 piece, plastic band glass lens globe
$150.00–$225.00 (C)

Socony Ethyl with Ethyl Trademark
Standard Oil Company
New York, New York
15", 3 piece, reproduction metal band,
original glass lens globe
$450.00 (B)

Sohio X-Tane
Standard Oil Company
Ohio
13½", 3 piece, glass band glass lens globe
(Lens in very poor condition, bidder essentially
paid $100.00 for the band and $10.00 for the
lens.)
$125.00 (C)

Solite Perfect Gasoline *globe*
Standard Oil of Indiana
16½", 3 piece, metal band glass lens globe
circa 1920s
$450.00–$900.00 (C)

Courtesy of Gene Sonnen

Standard Oil Crown *globe (blue)*
Standard Oil of Indiana
Original one piece glass crown shaped globe
with screw-on base
mint condition
$500.00–$700.00 (C)

Standard Oil Crown *globe (red & blue)*
Standard Oil of Indiana
One piece glass crown shaped globe (very early and very rare globe with raised lettering spelling "gasoline")
circa 1920s
$1,700.00–$2,000.00 (C)

Standard Oil Crown *globe*
One piece glass crown shaped globe (This globe is typical of an original washed-out crown globe. Beware of reproductions.)
$275.00–$400.00 (C)

Southern Marketer. Inc.
with map of Indiana and scenery picture globe
Independent Oil Company
13½", 3 piece, glass band with metal base glass lens globe
$1,150.00 (C)

Sovereign Service with double S logo at top
Independent Oil Companies
13½", 3 piece, yellow ripple glass band glass lens globe
Sovereign Service was made up of several independent
dealers such as Derby and Kanotex.
$950.00 (B)

Blue Sunoco Globe
Sun Oil Company
Philadelphia, Pennsylvania
15", 3 piece, metal band glass lens globe
$350.00–$500.00 (C)

Sunray Gasoline Globe
13½", 3 piece, orange plastic band glass lens globe
Sunray later combined with D–X to form D–X Sunray.
$350.00–$500.00 (C)

Super Flash with Ethyl logo globe
Crystal Flash Petroleum
Indianapolis, Indiana
13½", 3 piece, glass ripple band glass lens globe
$1,000.00–$1,200.00 (C)

Superior Gasoline Globe
15", 3 piece, metal band glass lens globe
$400.00–$500.00 (C)

Texaco Sky Chief with logo at bottom left
The Texas Company
Port Arthur, Texas
13", 3 piece, plastic band glass lens globe
$275.00–$325.00 (C)

Texaco Ethyl *with logo in center*
The Texas Company
Port Arthur, Texas
Notice the black edge around the green "T" in the center logo. This was used from 1936 into the 1940s when a white outline was adapted as shown in the bottom photo on page 69.
1 piece glass globe
$1,250.00–$1,400.00 (C)

Texaco Diesel Chief *globe (logo at top)*
The Texas Company
Port Arthur, Texas
13½", 3 piece, glass band glass lens globe
$400.00–$500.00 (C)

Transport Gasoline *globe*
Pennzoil Company
13½", 3 piece, glass band glass lens globe with screw–on base
$275.00–$350.00 (C)

Tri–State Super Motor (speed lettering)
Tri–State Refining
Kenova, West Virginia
13½", 3 piece, glass narrow band glass lens globe
$250.00–$300.00 (C)

Tydol globe
Tide Water Company
New York, New York
15", 3 piece, metal band glass lens
(cast face) globe
circa 1920s
$600.00–$850.00 (C)

Tydol with large red painted band around
circumference
Tide Water Oil Company
New York, New York
15", 3 piece, metal band glass lens globe
circa 1935–45
$325.00 (C)

Tidex globe
Tide Water Oil Company
New York, New York
16½", 3 piece, metal band glass lens globe
Tidex was Tide Water's third grade gasoline
$400.00–$500.00 (C)

Tydol with Ethyl Trademark in center
Tide Water Oil Company
New York, New York
13½", 3 piece, glass band glass lens globe
$750.00 (B)

Tydol with flying A
Tide Water Oil Company
New York, New York
13½", 3 piece, glass wide band glass lens globe
$400.00–$600.00 (C)

United Super Charged Gasoline
Red Wine Oil Company
13½", 3 piece, glass band glass lens globe
Original globe band should be plastic. Also
unusual is six colors on lens face.
$350.00–$450.00 (C)

Red Star Valvoline Gasoline Globe
Valvoline Oil Company
New York, New York
15", 3 piece, metal band glass lens globe
circa 1920s–1930s
$600.00–$900.00 (C)

Victoria with Ethyl logo
Victoria Oil Company
Texas
3 piece, plastic oval band glass lens globe
$225.00 (D)

Wadhams Metro Globe
13½", 3 piece, glass band glass lens globe
$300.00–$350.00 (C)

Courtesy of Gene Sonnen

Whitlock Super Gasoline *Ethyl globe*
13½", 3 piece, plastic band glass lens globe
$250.00 (C)

Courtesy of Gene Sonnen

White Eagle *globes*
Far left and far right are blunt nose or cut throat eagles
Second in from far left and second in from far right are full feather,
pointed nose style, Center is the "Crow" style
All are 1 piece glass eagle shaped globes
$900.00–$1,500.00 (value is for each of these globes) (C)

Xcel globe
Pure Oil Company
15", 3 piece, porcelain band glass
lens globe. Xcel was Pure Oil
Company's third grade gas
(relatively rare) $700.00–$850.00 (C)

Zephyr (speed letters) Supreme Ethyl logo globe
3 piece, plastic band glass lens globe
$225.00 (D)

Gene Sonnen's partial collection of globes. This display is a great example of a collector's desire to display a collection to its best advantage. Wiring all these globes to light up must have been a true labor of love for Gene!

PUMPS

During the 1950's and 60's when it came time to fill your gas tank you not only considered the price of a gallon of gas, but trading stamps, give away premiums like dinnerware, and perhaps most of all where you would receive the most prompt and courteous service! Of course in the earlier days of motoring, especially in rural areas, your options were reduced considerably. In fact a wise motorist would carry a can of gasoline with them, just in case the only station in a remote area was closed. In many instances the "station" consisted of a rolling gas cart or even a stationary gas drum with an attached hand crank. Small curb pumps began to appear at general stores. As traffic and the need for larger quantities of gas increased, petroleum companies responded with larger, heavier (much heavier!) brass pumping cylinders. Surrounded by the usual cast iron housings, these pumps were formidable pieces of equipment taking a strong will and stronger back to maneuver. Early Gilbert and Barker pumps (see page 82) took a small crane to move. Gradually the cast iron was replaced with sheet metal and the weight was reduced to a more respectable limit.

The motorist back then had little control over the accuracy of their purchase because these early pumps had no way of measuring gas as it was dispensed, and early automobiles used a dip stick to measure the quantity in the car's tank. The introduction of the visible cylinder pump addressed the problem. The customer could now see his purchase and, with the help of gallon markers attached to the side of the cylinder, was assured of an accurate delivery. Not wishing to lose their investment on existing pumps, manufacturers scurried to design visible attachments to convert these pre-visible pumps to state-of-the-art for this time period (see ad on page 104). Depending on gravity to deliver gas from the pump to the car, it was necessary for the measuring cylinder to be higher than the car's tank. For this reason pumps were tall, some over ten feet including the globe. The early visibles used a gate valve near the cylinder to open the flow of gas to the tank—the dry hose method of delivery. For this style of delivery the cylinders would be numbered from the bottom up. Later a nozzle with a built in valve would be patented and the cylinder could be filled and drained until the desired gallons were delivered—the wet hose method of

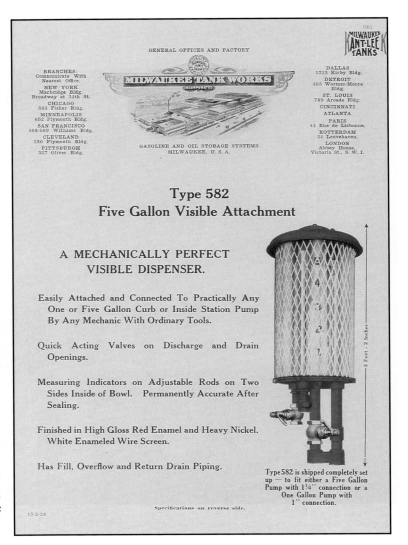

GENERAL OFFICES AND FACTORY

MILWAUKEE TANK WORKS
INCORPORATED

BRANCHES:
Communicate With
Nearest Office.
NEW YORK
Marbridge Bldg.
Broadway at 34th St.
CHICAGO
503 Fisher Bldg.
MINNEAPOLIS
652 Plymouth Bldg.
SAN FRANCISCO
508-509 Williams Bldg.
CLEVELAND
230 Plymouth Bldg.
PITTSBURGH
327 Oliver Bldg.

GASOLINE AND OIL STORAGE SYSTEMS
MILWAUKEE, U. S. A.

DALLAS
1313 Kirby Bldg.
DETROIT
403 Wormer-Moore
Bldg.
ST. LOUIS
789 Arcade Bldg.
CINCINNATI
ATLANTA
44 Rue de Lisbonne.
PARIS
ROTTERDAM
34 Leuvehaven.
LONDON
Abbey House,
Victoria St., S. W. I.

MILWAUKEE KANT-LEEK TANKS

Type 582
Five Gallon Visible Attachment

A MECHANICALLY PERFECT
VISIBLE DISPENSER.

Easily Attached and Connected To Practically Any
One or Five Gallon Curb or Inside Station Pump
By Any Mechanic With Ordinary Tools.

Quick Acting Valves on Discharge and Drain
Openings.

Measuring Indicators on Adjustable Rods on Two
Sides Inside of Bowl.   Permanently Accurate After
Sealing.

Finished in High Gloss Red Enamel and Heavy Nickel.
White Enameled Wire Screen.

Has Fill, Overflow and Return Drain Piping.

Type 582 is shipped completely set
up — to fit either a Five Gallon
Pump with 1¼" connection or a
One Gallon Pump with
1" connection.

15-2-24

Specifications on reverse side.

delivery. For this style of delivery the cylinders would be numbered from the top down. This is a feature to keep in mind when shopping for an accurately restored pump.

Visible cylinder pumps were offered with three methods of operation. One was the use of air pressure to force gas into the cylinder. A second method used an electric motor directly under the pump, and the third used a hand crank. The first method, air pressure, had its problems. The electric motor method made more than a few customers and attendants nervous because of the proximity of the electric motor to the explosive gasoline, and electricity was not available everywhere. The third method, hand cranking, could be used almost anywhere by anyone and became very popular. These hand crank pumps would continue to provide a service long after their life at the service station was over. They were just the thing for farm use. For this reason, many collectors have found these prize possessions in remote agricultural areas.

Since the maximum capacity for the non-visible brass cylinder pump was in most cases five gallons the first glass cylinders had a capacity of five gallons. This quantity was soon doubled to the standard ten gallons and some manufacturers introduced a fifteen gallon cylinder. Original glass cylinders are very rare. When shopping for a replacement cylinder always carry a tape measure since there were a number of diameter and height variations. When you do find one, be very careful handling it, they are extraordinarily fragile. Early dual cylinder five and ten gallon pumps have had a better survival rate in Canada, and can more easily be found there today.

It is generally agreed that visible pumps had their beginning due to mistrust, because of the inability to see the product. Because many early visible pumps had their gallon markers on the outside of the cylinder, they could be easily moved up and down and did little to alleviate the problem of not-so-honest dealers. As a result pump designers began placing the indicators inside the cylinder.

The use of visible pumps by the major producers was short-lived partly because the glass cylinder was fragile but primarily due to the continuing demand for faster, more accurate means of delivery. The advent of clockface electric pumps equipped with a sight glass was the next step in pump evolution. These pumps took over the market rapidly, except in areas not equipped with electricity. Variations of the clockface pump included the cash recorder—a pump with two dials on each side of the pump, recording the gallons with one indicator and the total dollars and cents sale with the other. Examples of this type of pump are extremely difficult to find today (page 92).

The invention of the mechanical pump computer with its digital readout for both quantity and price, and the ease of changing these amounts, pushed the clockface pump into the history books. Pumps caught up in the period of conversion to computer machinery may be found in either clockface or computer models. The Wayne model 60 is a good example. The mechanical computer pump reigned supreme for many years. The final blow to the these pumps came in the rapid advancement of technology (LED readout) and the Arab oil embargo pushing prices so high that the older mechanical computers had difficulty keeping up. As with all collectibles, items in our society today will some day be a treasured antique. Sometime in the distant future someone will proudly display their digital LED Tokheim pump with its remote control electronics as a unique collectible!

Trying to arrange this chapter alphabetically was a nightmare! Like the rest of this book, this chapter is set up alphabetically, with a small difference. Where there was an oil company shown on the pump, that is how it will be listed. But when there was no obvious oil company, it will be listed by the pump manufacturing company. Because this chapter is compiled this way, if you are looking for one pump in particular, you may have a little browsing to do!

Give Credit Where Credit Is Due

The pump restorations in this book all have one thing in common. Besides being great they were all completed by master craftsmen. An experienced collector will immediately recognize the quality that is apparent even in the photos. If you are new to this field of collecting you must keep in mind that pump restoration, just like classic auto restoration, is a true art form. You may find many claiming to "do pumps" but there are just a few real restoration artists. Listed below are a few of the artists who have helped with this chapter.

John Guildford a.k.a. Gas Pump Johnny has been restoring pumps for 18 years. And unlike some other restorers all of his completed pumps retain all their interior hardware.

John's Custom Fabrication, Inc. John remachines all of his pumps and when finished they are the envy of Swiss watchmakers.

Rob Vest was kind enough to furnish us with some before and after shots. Just seeing these photos will illustrate the transformation possible with quality restoration work.

Don Larson's pumps exhibit his obsession for minute details, as can also be seen in the miniature Texaco station pictured here.

Model Texaco station built by Don Larson features light up pump, globes, air meter, Texaco sign and office lighting. Approximatley 18" x 18".

John Romagnoli has not only helped us on this book, he has also featured his collection of rare and unusual pumps in many national publications.

Jerry and Sharron Goulet specialize in fifties pumps and computer rebuilding. Their pumps are restored to new working condition with rechroming and stainless polish work.

Nicky Fox, working on limited time for pump restoration, concentrates on rare and unusual pumps.

Bob Hull performs professional work which includes restoration of iron, brass and aluminum castings.

For all the true artists listed above: thanks and keep up the good work.

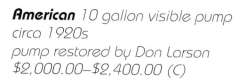

American 10 gallon visible pump
circa 1920s
pump restored by Don Larson
$2,000.00–$2,400.00 (C)

Amoco gasoline pump
Gilbarco Electric pump
circa 1950s
pump restored by John Guildford
$1,400.00–$1,500.00 (C)
(value includes original globe)

Courtesy of John Guildford

Courtesy of Don Larson

Ashland gasoline pump
Tokheim 10 gallon visible pump
$900.00–$1,200.00 (C)
(value is as-is condition)

Amoco gasoline pump
Wayne Dual Delivery Electric model 605-5 pump (original condition)
circa 1960s
$675.00 (D) (value includes reproduction globe)

Courtesy of Jerry & Sharron Goulet

Courtesy of Gene Sonnen

Courtesy of Rob Vest

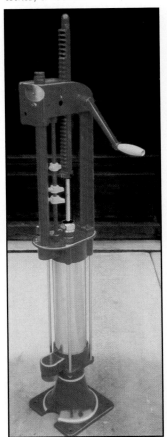

Bowser pre-visible
one gallon pump
pump restored by Rob Vest
$250.00–$400.00 (C)

Courtesy of Nicky Fox

Bowser gas cart with transfer can
$400.00–$500.00 (C)

Big Chief gasoline pump Wayne model 452
twin five gallon cylinders visible pump
circa 1924
restored by Nicky Fox
$4,500.00–$6,500.00 (C)
(value includes globe)

Bengal gasoline pump Bowser pre-visible "tower" model pump
circa 1912–1915
pump restored by John Guildford
$2,500.00–$2,700.00 (C)
(value does not include globe)

Courtesy of John Guildford

Courtesy of John Guildford

Bowser *pre-visible model 97 square sentry pump*
circa 1915
pump restored by John Guildford
$2,800.00–$3,200.00 (C)

Courtesy of Bob Petigrew

Bowser *pre-visible cast iron pump*
circa 1915–1920
pump restored by Bob Petigrew
$1,500.00–$1,800.00 (C)

Butler *clockface electric pump*
circa late 1920's, early 1930's
pump restored by Don Larson
$2,500.00–$2,900.00 (C)

Cities Service *pump*
Bennett Clockface Electric pump
circa 1930's
$1,800.00–$2,400.00 (C)

Courtesy of Don Larson

Courtesy of John Guildford

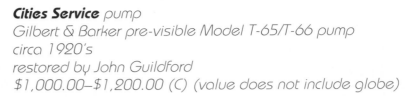

Cities Service pump
Gilbert & Barker pre-visible Model T-65/T-66 pump
circa 1920's
restored by John Guildford
$1,000.00–$1,200.00 (C) (value does not include globe)

Courtesy of John Hasken

Cities Service pump
Wayne Model 60 Electric pump
(original condition)
circa late 1930's–early 1940's
$600.00–$700.00 (C)

Clipper pump
Wayne "Tall Ten"
10 gallon visible pump
restored by John Romagnoli
$3,000.00–$5,000.00 (C)
(value does not include globe)

Courtesy of John Romagnoli

It's the Best Motor Oil known to Science

(Partial view of the enormous new lubricating oil plant at Lake Charles, La., where this great new oil is processed.)

"ANTI-FOULING" OIL made by the Remarkable new "HEART-CUT" PROCESS

This new oil—the best known to science... gives you a cleaner engine...more economy ...minimum carbon residue.

It's here now! The remarkable motor oil from the giant new $42,000,000 lubricating oil plant at Lake Charles, La. The plant that's been the big talk of the oil industry for months.

New Premium Koolmotor is made by the unique "Heart-Cut" Process which retains only the choicest part of the finest crudes. *It's so superior that in recent engine tests it outscored nine other major premium motor oils.* No wonder Premium Koolmotor is better in every way! Cleans better, seals better, cools better and fights acid, sludge and corrosion far more effectively. Switch to this remarkable new oil today.

start saving Dollars today...stop at

CITIES △ SERVICE

194

SUPER SERVICE Station

Courtesy of Don Larson

Conoco pump
Fry Model 87 10 gallon visible pump
circa 1920's
restored by Don Larson
$2,600.00–$2,900.00 (C)
(value does not include globe)

CO-OP pump
Tokheim "Salesmaker" Model 36 pump
circa 1930's
restored by Nicky Fox
$4,000.00–$5,000.00 (C)
(value includes globe)

Correct Measure gas pump
$600.00–$800.00 (C)
(value is as-is condition)

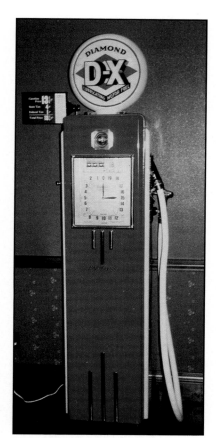

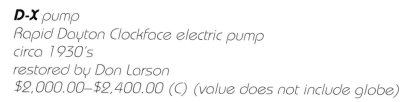

Courtesy of Don Larson

D-X pump
Rapid Dayton Clockface electric pump
circa 1930's
restored by Don Larson
$2,000.00–$2,400.00 (C) (value does not include globe)

Courtesy of John Guildford

D-X pump
Bowser Xacto Sentry Clockface pump
restored by Rob Vest
$3,000.00–$5,000.00 (C)
(value does not include globe)

Courtesy of Rob Vest

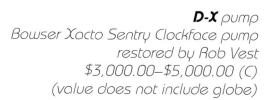

Esso pump (repo Chevrolet globe)
Bennett Electric pump
circa 1930's–1940's
restored by John Guildford
$1,200.00–$1,400.00 (C)
(value does not include globe)

Esso *pump*
Wayne Model 60 Clockface Electric pump
circa 1930s
restored by John Guildford
$2,800.00 (D)

Esso *pump*
Gilbert & Barker five gallon visible pump
circa 1920s
$1,500.00–$1,800.00 (C)
(value does not include globe)

Courtesy of John Guildford

Courtesy of John Guildford

Esso *pump*
Martin & Schwartz Electric Model 80 pump
circa 1940s–1950s
restored by John Guildford
$1,200.00–$1,400.00 (C)

Fry *10 gallon visible pump*
circa 1920s
$700.00–$950.00 (C)
(value is as-is condition)

Courtesy of John Guildford

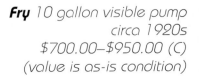

Gilmore *gasoline pump*
Wayne Model 60 pump
circa 1937 (restored to original
working condition)
restored by Jerry & Sharron Goulet
$2,500.00–$3,000.00 (C)
(value includes reproduction globe)

Gulf *gasoline pump*
National electric model 360 pump
circa 1950s
restored by John Guildford
$1,600.00–$1,800.00 (C)
(value does not include globe)

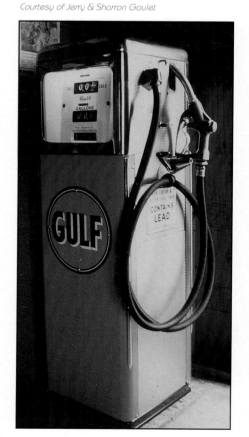

Gulf *gasoline pump*
Gilbert & Barker clockface electric pump
circa 1930s
restored by John Guildford
$1,500.00–$1,800.00 (C)
(value does not include globe)

Gulf *gasoline pump*
Bennett Electric Model 748 pump
circa 1966
(restored to new working condition)
restored by Jerry & Sharron Goulet
$750.00–$950.00 (C)

Gulf *gasoline pump*
Rush ten gallon visible "stove pipe" model pump
circa 1920s
restored by John Guildford
$1,900.00–$2,200.00 (C)
(value does not include globe)

Gulf *gasoline pump*
Erie Electric pump
circa 1950s
restored by John Guildford
$1,200.00 (D)
(value does not include globe)

Gulf *gasoline pump*
Shotwell pre-visible Model 575 pump
circa 1920s
$1,100.00–$1,300.00 (C)
(value does not include globe)

Gulf *gasoline pump*
National Duplex pump
(very desirable)
restored by Rob Vest
$6,500.00–$8,500.00 (C)
(value does not include globe)

Indian *gasoline pump*
Tokheim 36B tall electric pump
circa 1930s–1940s
restored by Don Larson
$2,400.00–$2,800.00 (C)
(value does not include globe)

Inglis *pre-visible pump*
circa 1915
restored by Nicky Fox
$1,500.00–$2,500.00 (C)

Courtesy of Nicky Fox

Indian *gasoline pump*
Gilbert & Barker ten gallon visible pump
(blue cylinder makes this pump desirable
along with the porcelain Indian Pump sign.)
$475.00–$575.00 (C) (value is as-is)

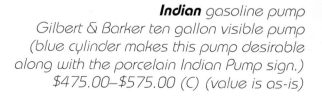

Kanotex *gasoline pump*
American ten gallon visible Model 2487-B pump
restored by John's Custom Fabrication, Inc.
$3,000.00–$8,000.00 (C) (value includes globe)

Courtesy of John's Custom Fabrication, Inc.

Kanotex *gasoline pump*
Bowser Xacto Sentry clockface electric pump
circa late 1920s–early 1930s
restored by John's Custom Fabrication, Inc.
$3,000.00–$8,000.00 (C) (value includes globe)

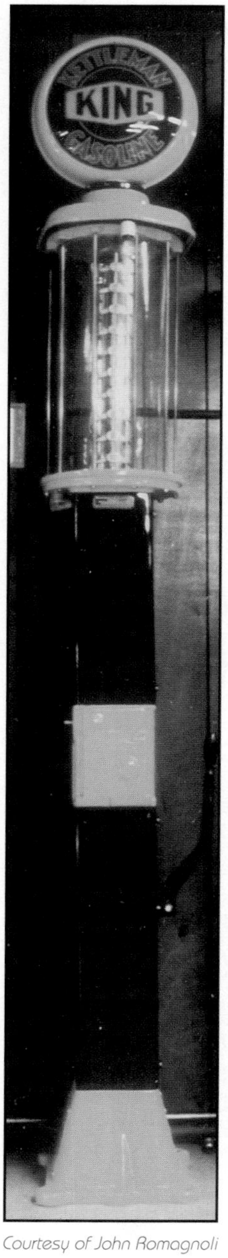

Courtesy of John Romagnoli

Kettleman King *gasoline pump*
Bowser ten gallon visible pump
circa 1920s
restored by John Romagnoli
$3,000.00–$5,000.00 (C)
(value does not include globe)

Courtesy of John Guildford

Milwaukee *cash recorder*
(rare) electric pump
circa 1930s
$1,950.00–$2,350.00 (C)
(value is as-is condition)

Mobilgas Special *pump*
National "roll-top"
A38 tall electric pump
$2,000.00–$2,400.00 (C)
(value does not include globe)

Courtesy of Don Larson

Mobilgas *pump*
Wayne 60 narrow body electric pump
circa late 1930s–early1940s
restored by Don Larson
$2,000.00–$2,400.00 (C)
(value does not include globe)

Mobilgas *pump*
Bowser pre-visible, crank, curb pump with globe holder
circa late 1915
restored by Don Larson
$2,000.00–$2,200.00 (C)
(value does not include globe)

Courtesy of Don Larson

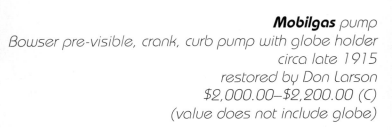

Mobilgas Special *pump*
Bennett tall electric pump
circa late 1930s–early 1940s
restored by Don Larson
$1,400.00–$1,800.00 (C)
(value does not include globe)

Courtesy of Don Larson

Mobiloil *pump*
American lubster pump featuring glass cylinder
restored by Don Larson
$1,800.00–$2,000.00 (C)

Courtesy of Gene Sonnen

Courtesy of Don Larson

Courtesy of Don Larson

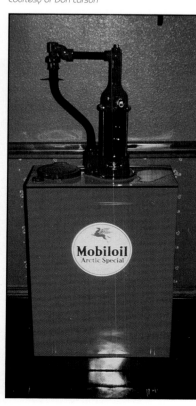

Mobilgas Special *pump*
Tokheim porcelain body electric pump
circa 1950s
restored by Gene Sonnen
$575.00–$700.00 (C)
(value does not include globe)

Mobiloil *pump*
Erie lubster pump
restored by Don Larson
$500.00–$600.00 (C)

Courtesy of Jerry & Sharron Goulet

Courtesy of John Guildford

Mobilgas pump
Bennett electric model 966 pump
circa 1955
(restored to new working condition)
restored by Jerry & Sharron Goulet
$1,600.00–$1,800.00 (C)
(value includes reproduction globe)

Mobilgas pump
Wayne ten gallon visible model 515
pump equipped with high base
(original cylinder)
circa 1927
(restored to new working condition)
restored by Jerry & Sharron Goulet
$2,800.00–$3,200.00 (C)
(value includes globe)

Courtesy of Jerry & Sharron Goulet

Mobilegas Special pump
Martin & Schwartz with light-up Mobilgas
Special lettering model 80 pump
circa 1940s–1950s
restored by John Guildford
$1,200.00–$1,400.00 (C)

Mobilegas pump
Wayne model 60 pump
circa 1930s–1940s
restored by John Guildford
$1,750.00–$1,900.00 (C)
(value does not include globe)

Courtesy of John Guildford

Mobilgas *pump*
Wayne short electric pump
circa 1950s
restored by John Guildford
$1,350.00 (D)
(value does not include globe)

Mobilgas Special *pump*
Gilbert & Barker tall electric pump
circa 1940s
restored by John Guildford
$1,100.00–$1,200.00 (C)
(value does not include globe)

Mobilgas *pump*
Bennett short electric pump
circa 1950s
restored by Don Larson
$1,200.00–$1,500.00 (C)
(value does not include globe)

Mobilgas *pump*
Martin & Schwartz electric
model 70 pump
circa 1940s
$475.00–$600.00 (C)
(value includes globe)

Musgo *gasoline pump*
Wayne model 60 electric pump
circa 1930s–1940s
restored by John Guildford
$1,750.00–$1,950.00 (C)
(value does not include globe)

National Simplex *clockface pump*
circa late 1920s–early 1930s
restored by Don Larson
$3,400.00–$3,900.00 (C)
(See restored pump on bottom of page 88)

Courtesy of John Guildford

Courtesy of Don Larson

National Duplex *pump*
circa 1930s
very desirable
$2,800.00–$3,800.00 (C)
(See restored pump pictured on page 88.)

Courtesy of Rob Vest

Courtesy of Bob Hull

National Duplex *clockface pump*
circa 1930s
restored by Bob Hull
$6,500.00–$8,500.00 (C)

Courtesy of Rob Vest

Wayne *model 60 narrow body pump*
circa 1940s
(compare with next pump)
$600.00–$750.00 (C)
(value does not include globe)

(No Company)
Early one quart kerosene or gasoline curb
pump
circa 1910–1915
restored by John & Cindy Ogle
$125.00–$225.00 (C)

Courtesy of John & Cindy Ogle

Courtesy of Rob Vest

NevrNox Gasoline *pump*
Wayne model 60 narrow body pump
circa 1940s
restored by Rob Vest
$1,800.00–$2,400.00 (C)
(value does not include globe)
(Notice value difference between restored
and unrestored pumps.)

Ottawa *ten gallon visible pump*
circa 1920s
restored by John Guildford
$2,500.00–$2,700.00 (C)
(value does not include globe)

Courtesy of John Guildford

Pennzoil *gasoline pump*
Erie Clockface electric pump
circa 1930s
$1,800.00–$2,000.00 (C)

Courtesy of John Guildford

Courtesy of John Guildford

Pennzoil *gasoline pump*
Erie Clockface electric pump
circa 1930s
restored by John Guildford
$1,800.00–$2,000.00 (C)
(value does not
include globe)

Pennzoil *gasoline pump*
Gilbert & Barker pre-visible pump
circa 1920s
restored by John Guildford
$1,200.00–$1,400.00 (C) (value does not include globe)

Courtesy of John Guildford

Courtesy of John's Custom Fabrications, Inc

Phillips 66 *gasoline pump*
Bowser Xacto Sentry Clockface electric pump
circa late 1920s–early 1930s
restored by John's Custom Fabrications, Inc.
$3,000.00–$8,000.00 (C)
(value includes globe)

Courtesy of Don Larson

Phillips 66 *gasoline pump*
Gilbarco tall electric pump
circa 1940s–1950s
restored by Don Larson
$1,300.00–$1,600.00 (C)
(value does not include globe)

Phillips 66 *gasoline pump*
Gilbarco tall electric pump
circa 1940s
$1,300.00–$1,600.00 (C)
(value does not include globe)

Courtesy of Don Larson

Phillips 66 *gasoline pump*
Bennett tall electric pump
circa 1930s–1940s
restored by Don Larson
$1,500.00–$1,900.00 (C)

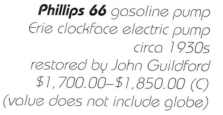

Courtesy of John Guildford

Phillips 66 *gasoline pump*
Erie clockface electric pump
circa 1930s
restored by John Guildford
$1,700.00–$1,850.00 (C)
(value does not include globe)

Courtesy of Nicky Fox

Phillips 66 *gasoline pump*
Fry Model 17 five gallon visible pump
(early model with cast iron base)
circa 1920s
restored by Nicky Fox
$1,750.00–$2,500.00 (C)
(value includes globe)

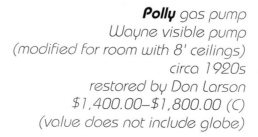

Courtesy of Don Larson

Polly *gas pump*
Wayne visible pump
(modified for room with 8' ceilings)
circa 1920s
restored by Don Larson
$1,400.00–$1,800.00 (C)
(value does not include globe)

Polly *gas pump*
Bennett tall electric pump
circa 1930s–1940s
restored by Don Larson
$1,500.00–$1,800.00 (C)
(value does not include globe)

Polly *gas pump*
Fry visible pump (modified to use in
room with 8' ceilings)
circa 1920s
restored by Don Larson
$1,400.00–$1,800.00 (C)
(value does not include globe)

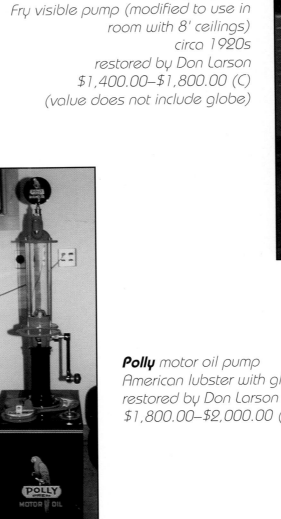

Polly *motor oil pump*
American lubster with glass cylinder pump
restored by Don Larson
$1,800.00–$2,000.00 (C)

Courtesy of Don Guildford

Polly *gas pump*
Bennett clockface electric pump
circa 1930s
restored by Don Guildford
$1,500.00–$1,800.00 (C)
(value does not include globe)

Red Crown *gasoline pump*
Wayne ten gallon visible model 515
pump (equipped with high base)
circa 1927
(restored to original working condition
with original glass cylinder)
restored by Jerry & Sharron Goulet
$2,800.00–$3,200.00 (C)
(value includes globe)

Courtesy of Don Larson

Courtesy of Don Larson

Red Crown *gasoline pump*
American tall electric pump
circa 1940s
restored by Don Larson
$1,500.00–$1,800.00 (C)

Rapidayton *pre-visible crank pump*
circa 1915
restored by Don Larson
$2,000.00–$2,200.00 (C)

Presenting...

The *first* Clinical
Test-Proved High Visibility Dial

BEFORE AND AFTER DELIVERY

DRIVE SAFELY

$0.00 PURCHASE
Rapidayton
THE DAYTON PUMP & MFG. CO., DAYTON, OHIO

0.0 0/10 GALLONS
DISCHARGE RATE FULL FLOW TO 5 GAL. PER MIN.

2 | 8 | 1/2
PER GALLON • TAXES INCLUDED

Patent applied for

HERE IS A DIAL that has been developed in consultation with men skilled in physiological optics. Their clinical tests determined the proper relative proportion of black and white to give the utmost *visibility* and *readability*—at any serving length.

It is a long known scientific optical fact that *too much black* tones down illumination and, in the design of a dial, the proper balance between black and white areas must be carefully maintained to insure utmost perceivability. But never until now have the proper proportions been scientifically determined for a gasoline dispensing pump.

With this RAPIDAYTON dial, your customers and attendants no longer have to squint to see the figures, which *really stand out*. Truly, it is America's most easily read dial. It safeguards your transactions and speeds up your service. A "must" for use with extension type hose. Write for details.

Rapidayton
COMPUTING PUMPS

THE DAYTON PUMP & MFG. COMPANY • DAYTON, OHIO

Red Crown *gasoline pump*
Tokheim clockface electric model 850 pump
circa 1930s
restored by John Guildford
$1,800.00–$2,100.00 (C)
(value does not include globe)

Courtesy of John Guildford

Courtesy of John Guildford

Richfield *gasoline pump*
Row electric pump
circa 1930s
restored by John Guildford
$1,300.00–$1,600.00 (C)
(value does not include globe)

Red Crown *gasoline pump*
Wayne model 70 tall electric pump
circa 1940s
$1,100.00–$1,250.00 (C)
(value does not include globe)

Richfield gasoline pump
Bowser Xacto Sentry clockface electric pump
circa late 1920s–early 1930s
restored by John's Custom Fabrication, Inc.
$3,000.00–$8,000.00 (C)
(value includes globe)

Courtesy of of John Guildford

Richfield Ethyl gasoline pump
National clockface electric model A pump
circa 1930s
restored by John Guildford
$1,900.00–$2,300.00 (C)
(value does not include globe)

Courtesy of John's Custom Fabrication, Inc.

Richfield gasoline pump
Ottawa ten gallon visible pump
circa 1920s
restored by John Guildford
$2,500.00–$2,700.00 (C)
(value does not include globe)

Courtesy of John Guildford

Sharmeter clockface electric model 513A pump
circa 1930s
close-up of rare pump
$2,300.00–$2,500.00 (C)

Courtesy of John Guildford

Courtesy of Don Larson

Shell gasoline pump
Tokheim model 36B tall electric pump
circa late 1930s–early 1940s
restored by Don Larson
$2,400.00–$2,800.00 (C)
(value does not include globe)

Courtesy of Don Larson

Courtesy of Don Larson

Shell gasoline pump
Wayne 519C ten gallon visible
pump
circa 1920s
restored by Don Larson
$2,400.00–$2,600.00 (C)
(value does not include globe)

Shell gasoline pump
Rapid Dayton clockface electric pump
circa late 1920s–early 1930s
restored by Don Larson
$2,000.00–$2,450.00 (C) (value does not include globe)

Shell *motor oil pump*
American lubster with glass cylinder pump
restored by Don Larson
$1,800.00–$2,000.00 (C)

Shell *motor oil pump cart*
unrestored oil pump cart with three grades of oil
(most carts have only two)
$375.00–$450.00 (C)

Shell *gasoline pump*
Bennett electric model 646 pump
circa 1940
(restored to new working condition)
restored by Jerry & Sharron Goulet
$1,900.00–$2,200.00 (C)
(value includes reproduction globe)

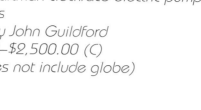

Shell *gasoline pump*
St. Louis Hartman clockface electric pump
circa 1930s
restored by John Guildford
$2,300.00–$2,500.00 (C)
(value does not include globe)

Shell *gasoline pump*
A. O. Smith electric model L-1 pump
circa 1950s
restored by John Guildford
$1,000.00–$1,200.00 (C)
(value does not include globe)

Sinclair H-C *gasoline pump*
Bennett tall electric pump
circa 1940s
$1,100.00–$1,300.00 (C)
(value does not include globe)

Signal *gasoline pump*
Fry ten gallon visible pump
equipped with gravel shield
restored by Rob Vest
$2,000.00–$2,800.00 (C)
(value does not include globe)

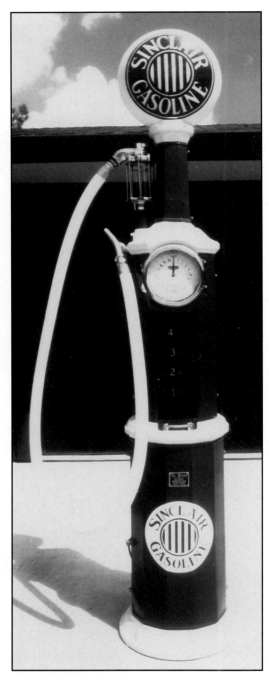

Courtesy of Rob Vest

Sinclair *gasoline pump*
National Simplex pump
restored by Rob Vest
$5,000.00–$8,000.00 (C)
(value does not include globe)

Sinclair gasoline pump
Bennett tall electric pump
circa late 1930s–early1940s
restored by Don Larson
$1,500.00–$1,850.00 (C)
(value does not include globe)

Courtesy of Don Larson

Sinclair gasoline pump
Wayne short electric pump
circa 1940s–1950s
restored by Don Larson
$1,200.00–$1,400.00 (C)
(value does not include globe)

Courtesy of Don Larson

Courtesy of Don Larson

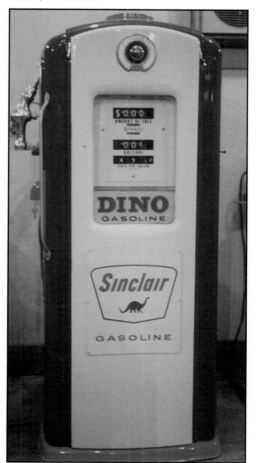

Sinclair gasoline pump
Bennett short electric pump
circa 1950s
restored by Don Larson
$1,200.00–$1,500.00 (C)

Sinclair opaline double pump lubster
$2,000.00 (C)

Courtesy of Jerry & Sharron Goulet

Sinclair gasoline pump
Bennett model 966 electric pump
circa 1955
(restored to new working condition)
restored by Jerry & Sharron Goulet
$1,700.00–$1,850.00 (C)
(value includes globe)

Courtesy of Jerry & Sharron Goulet

Sinclair gasoline pump
Wayne electric model 70 pump
circa 1947
(restored to new working condition)
restored by Jerry & Sharron Goulet
$1,800.00–$2,000.00 (C)

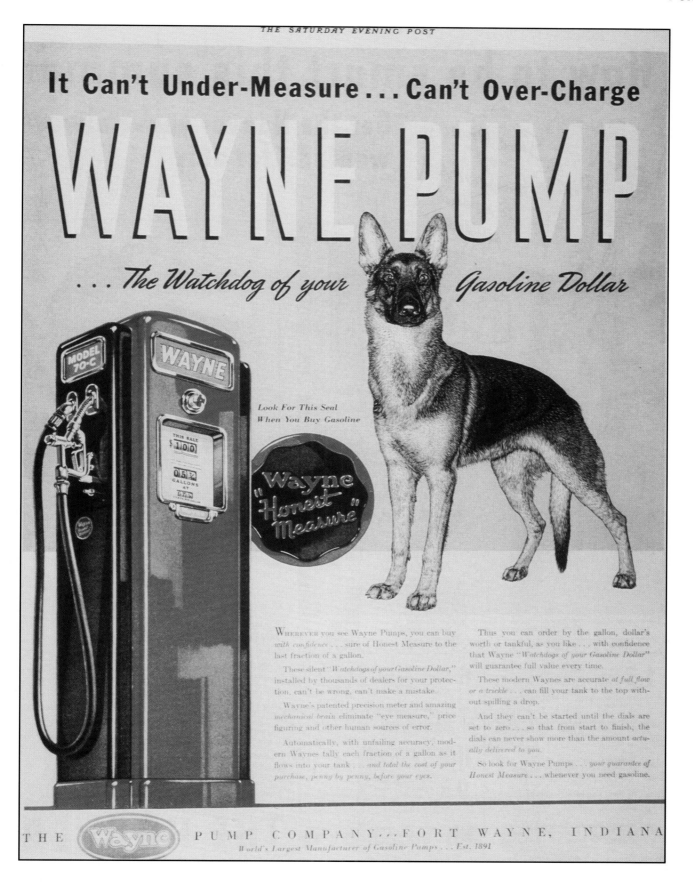

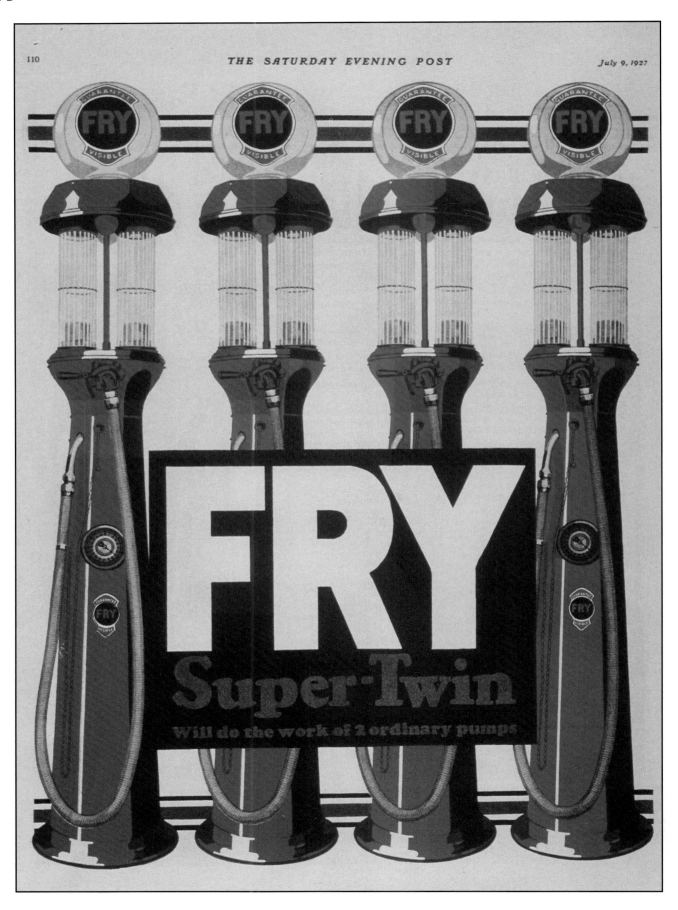

110   THE SATURDAY EVENING POST   July 9, 1927

FRY
Super-Twin
Will do the work of 2 ordinary pumps

Gasoline Sellers—!

The attention and interest of the entire gasoline industry is focused on the amazing array of advanced features incorporated in the Fry Super-Twin—the latest and greatest achievement ever offered in a gasoline pump.

Continuous flow—1 to 1000 gallons without stopping. *That gains gallonage!*

Every gallon measured visibly. *That gains gallonage!*

Every gallon measured with positive accuracy. *That gains gallonage!*

Elimination of the wet hose evil—Control at Nozzle. *That gains gallonage!*

Every gallon is recorded. *That gains gallonage!*

Every measured gallon is positively delivered. *That gains gallonage!*

It is power-operated and has pressure discharge. *That gains gallonage!*

The speed is amazing. *That gains gallonage!*

The design is unusually beautiful. *That gains gallonage!*

What is probably one of the greatest single contributions towards the further development and betterment of the thousands of already excellently equipped and well-managed gasoline filling stations, is the introduction of America's newest gasoline pump—the Fry Super-Twin.

Knowing the puzzling problems of every gasoline station owner, Fry undertook the responsibility of developing a more advanced pump which would make marketing of gasoline simpler, speedier, snappier, more attractive and more profitable.

At last this new pump is ready! For the development and perfection of the astonishing Fry Super-Twin eliminates in a most sweeping manner practically every single problem that has ever confronted you in connection with the sale of gasoline. Think that over—then read on!

This new and advanced pump is truly the answer to every pump buyer's dream.

Never before in the history of the entire pump industry has a pump been offered in which are incorporated so many refinements, each one of which is specially designed as a profit-producing aid to your business.

Already the more thoughtful buyers in all parts of the country are installing this latest pump. Now more than ever, Fry is recognized as the outstanding authority on service-station equipment.

The Fry Super-Twin, like all modern inventions, is a great aid to both the buyer and seller. It gives the buyer of gasoline —the motorist—faster, more economical, always accurate service. It gives the seller an opportunity to widen his business, increase his profits, and to make himself known as the most progressive, most alert and most deserving filling-station operator in his vicinity.

Write today for descriptive literature.

Now more than ever motorists will buy from a Fry!

GUARANTEE LIQUID MEASURE COMPANY
ROCHESTER, PENNSYLVANIA
FRY EQUIPMENT COMPANY, LIMITED, 10 King Street East, TORONTO, ONT.

"Always Accurate"

Sinclair *gasoline pump*
Fry ten gallon visible pump
$1,300.00–$1,600.00 (C)
(value does not include globe)

Sinclair *gasoline pump*
Erie electric pump
circa 1950s
restored by John Guildford
$1,000.00–$1,350.00 (C)
(value does not include globe)

Socony *gasoline pump*
Gilbert & Barker pre-visible pump
circa 1917
$1,000.00–$1,200.00 (C)
(value does not include globe)

Blue Sunoco *gasoline pump*
Wayne electric Blend-O-Matic model 511 pump
very good original condition
circa 1958
$475.00–$775.00 (C)
(value includes reproduction globe)

Blue Sunoco *gasoline pump*
Gilbarco electric pump
circa 1950s
restored by John Guildford
$1,100.00–$1,200.00 (C)
(value does not include globe)

Blue Sunoco *gasoline pump*
Tokheim clockface electric pump
circa 1930s
restored by John Guildford
$1,800.00–$2,400.00 (C)
(value does not include globe)

Texaco *gasoline pump*
Coin-A-Matic Model A ten gallon visible
pump
circa 1929
restored by John Romagnoli
$4,000.00–$5,500.00 (C)
(value does not include globe)

Courtesy of John's Custom Fabrication, Inc.

Texaco *gasoline pump*
Bowser Xacto Sentry Clockface electric pump
circa 1920s–1930s
restored by John's Custom Fabrication, Inc.
$3,000.00–$8,000.00 (C)
(value includes globe)

Courtesy of Don Larson

View from the front

Texaco motor oil pump
Tokheim lubster pump with dual dispensers
restored by Don Larson
$2,000.00 (C)

View from the back

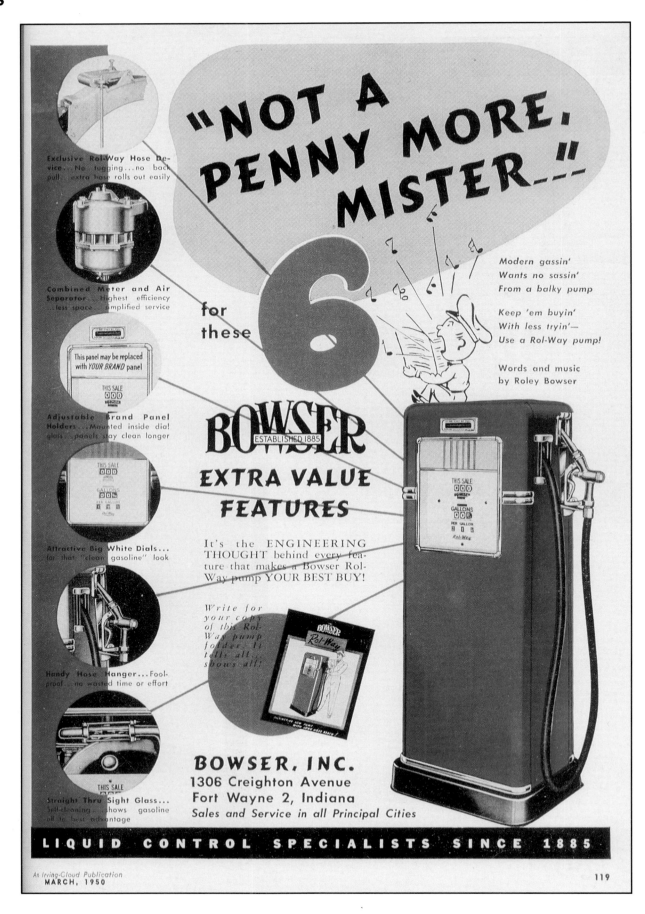

METER PUMP READING RECORD		
PUMP	No. 1	No. 2
CLOSING	500276	920922 746
OPENING	500050	920663
GAL. SOLD	226	259
AMOUNT	61.39	

The Best Pump
is the biggest bargain !

In gasoline pumps the best pump is the biggest bargain. For a few dollars' saving in purchase price may be only a temporary advantage quickly offset by high maintenance expense, inaccuracy, pump failure and costly "down" time. Tokheim pumps are competitively priced and superior in value. Don't be misled by so-called "bargains". Buy the pumps you can depend on. Buy Tokheims.

E-Z-Fill Model 39 L-EZ. 14 feet of hose when needed. Half is concealed. Easy to pull out and retract. Hose Reel and exterior hose types (Retrēv-A-Hose) also available.

BIGGEST VALUE BY FAR !

QUALITY **TOKHEIM** THE 4-SEASON PUMP

TOKHEIM OIL TANK AND PUMP CO.
DESIGNERS AND BUILDERS OF SUPERIOR EQUIPMENT
FORT WAYNE 1   FOR 49 YEARS   INDIANA

An Irving-Cloud Publication
MARCH, 1950

3

Texaco Fire Chief *gasoline pump*
Bowser tall electric pump
circa 1940s
restored by Don Larson
$1,200.00–$1,600.00 (C)
(value does not include globe)

Texaco *gasoline pump*
Gilbert & Barker model
T-65/T-66 pump
circa 1917–1920
restored by John Guildford
$1,000.00–$1,200.00 (C)
(value does not include globe)

Texaco Sky Chief *gasoline pump*
Tokheim electric model 39 pump
circa 1950s
restored by John Guildford
$1,100.00–$1,300.00 (C)
(value does not include globe)

Texaco Ethyl *gasoline pump*
Tokheim clockface electric "Volumeter" model 850 pump
circa 1930
restored to new working condition
restored by Jerry & Sharron Goulet
$2,500.00–$4,000.00 (C)
(value includes reproduction globe)

Texaco Sky Chief *gasoline pump*
Tokheim electric model 300 pump
circa 1956
(restored to new working condition)
restored by Jerry & Sharron Goulet
$1,600.00–$1,800.00 (C) (value
includes reproduction globe)

Courtesy of Jerry & Sharron Goulet

Courtesy of John Guildford

Courtesy of Jerry & Sharron Goulet

Texaco Sky Chief *gasoline pump*
Gilbert & Barker clockface electric pump
circa 1930s
restored by John Guildford
$1,800.00–$2,000.00 (C)

Texaco Sky Chief *gasoline pump*
Bennett electric model 966 pump
circa 1950s
restored by John Guildford
$1,100.00–$1,250.00 (C)
(value does not include globe)

Courtesy of John Guildford

Texaco *gasoline pump*
Bowser Square Sentry pre-visible pump
circa 1915–1920
restored by Nicky Fox
$2,500.00–$3,500.00 (C)
(value includes globe)

Courtesy of Nicky Fox

Texaco *gasoline pump*
Gilbert & Barker clockface electric pump
circa 1930s
restored by Nicky Fox
$1,700.00–$2,000.00 (C) (value includes globe)

Courtesy of Nicky Fox

Texaco gasoline pump
Wayne ten gallon visible pump
circa 1920s
restored by Rob Vest
$1,800.00–$2,800.00 (C)
(value does not include globe)

(notice the difference in price and
condition of these two pumps)

Wayne ten gallon visible pump
(unrestored with good cylinder)
circa 1920s
$700.00–$800.00 (C)

Texaco Ethyl gasoline pump
Fry Model 117 ten gallon visible pump
circa 1920s
restored by John's Custom Fabrication, Inc.
$3,000.00–$8,000.00 (C)
(value does not include globe)

Tokheim Model 34ß *electric pump*
circa 1930s
$500.00–$750.00 (C)

Tokheim 850 *clockface electric pump*
circa 1930s
restored by Don Larson
$2,000.00–$2,450.00 (C)

Tydol Flying A *gasoline pump*
Tokheim Model 36 electric pump
circa 1930s
restored by Gene Sonnen
$1,200.00–$1,600.00 (C)
(value does not include globe)

Tokheim *clockface electric pump*
circa 1930s
unrestored with surface rust
$700.00–$850.00 (C)

Tydol Flying A *gasoline pump*
Bowser Xacto Sentry clockface electric pump
circa 1930s
restored by John Guildford
$2,000.00–$2,400.00 (C)
(value does not include globe)

Tydol Flying A *gasoline pump*
Bowser Xacto Sentry clockface electric pump
circa 1930s
restored by John Guildford
$2,000.00–$2,400.00 (C)
(value does not include globe)

Tydol Flying A *gasoline pump*
Fry five gallon visible model 17 pump
circa 1920s
restored by John Guildford
$1,900.00–$2,200.00 (C)
(value does not include globe)

Tydol Flying A *gasoline pump*
National Electric Model 360 pump
circa 1950s
restored by John Guildford
$1,200.00–$1,400.00 (C)

Tydol *gasoline pump*
Gilbert & Barker pre-visible pump
circa 1920s
$1,300.00–$1,450.00 (C)
(value includes globe)

Tydol Flying A *gasoline pump*
Erie clockface electric pump
circa 1930s
restored by John Guildford
$1,900.00–$2,200.00 (C)
(value does not include globe)

John, better known as Gas-Pump Johnny.

Courtesy of John Romagnoli

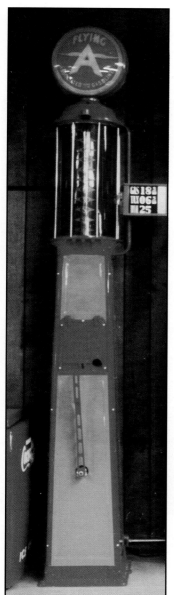

Courtesy of John Romagnoli

Tydol Flying A *gasoline pump*
Butler Model 61 ten gallon visible pump
circa 1920s
restored by John Romagnoli
$3,000.00–$5,000.00 (C)
(value does not include globe)

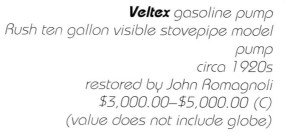

Veltex *gasoline pump*
Rush ten gallon visible stovepipe model
pump
circa 1920s
restored by John Romagnoli
$3,000.00–$5,000.00 (C)
(value does not include globe)

Velvet 98 *gasoline pump*
American Electric Model 700 pump
circa 1938
with rare milk glass dome top and
original pump signs
$2,500.00–$3,200.00 (C)

Courtesy of Jerry & Sharron Goulet

Courtesy of John Guildford

Wayne model 60 electric clockface pump
$800.00–$900.00 (C)

Wayne curb pump
detail picture of interior
circa 1915–1925
restored by Don Larson
$1,800.00–$2,000.00 (C)

Courtesy of Don Larson

Wayne model 60 pump
This is a much sought after pump due in part to its Art Deco styling. This pump is priced as shown, when restored expect to pay ten times this amount.
$300.00 (C)

Made in five and ten
gallon capacities—
both labeled by the
Underwriters' Lab-
oratories.

FRY
Visible Pump
Always Accurate

Wayne *gas cart*
restored by Don Larson
$2,000.00–$2,400.00 (C)

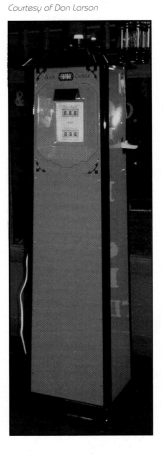

Wayne model 40 *electric pump*
circa 1930s
restored by Don Larson
$2,000.00–$2,400.00 (C)

White Rose No Knock *pump*
Wayne model 861 clockface electric pump
restored by John's Custom Fabrication, Inc.
$3,000.00–$8,000.00 (C)
(value includes globe)

SIGNS

Since the dawn of time when Oog got Ug's attention by drawing on the cave wall, people have been trying to get each other's attention with signs. Signs— love'em or hate'em— they're necessary for life as we know it. Early merchants, realizing they could sell their products if they could get people into their caves, or stores, erected signs at a head spinning rate.

Signs can be as simple as a message on paper, or as elaborate as neon on porcelain. Some are made of waxed cardboard, while others can be wood, canvas, cloth, tin, or metal. And all with varying degrees of artwork. Some are lit from external sources while others are self-illuminating.

As you drive down the street at night the chances are most of the illumination will be from advertising signs. Some of these will be flashing while others will have a constant light. Neon has been a favorite of advertisers because of its high visibility and its ability to cut through fog better than most other light sources.

As you look at a sign with an eye toward buying there are some questions to ask yourself. What material was used in construction? Does it have a flange mounting or does it hang from an arm, or mount on a flat surface? Is it one or two sided? Does it light up? If so what is the source of illumination? Does the light source work? What condition is the sign? A lot of people who price their wares don't read the part of a value guide that says these prices are for good quality pieces. So if someone prices you a porcelain sign in fair condition at a mint price, it's too much. Don't pay for the piece until the condition and price match. As a general rule porcelain and neon signs will command the higher prices. Porcelain signs required a great deal of skill and some luck to turn out good. I won't go into the complete process here but it involved stenciling the surface. A mixture of powdered glass and other materials would be sprayed on the surface. Then it would have to be fired in an oven. Each color added required an additional firing. This is the condensed version of a fairly complicated process. Neon came along later and is produced when an electrical charge is passed through a special gas enclosed in a clear tube.

I could go on but this is only supposed to be an introduction to signs. When I part with hard earned money for a sign the main criterion I use is—does it appeal to me? If it does I try to keep the other things, such as condition and availability, in mind. So my advice to you is simple: If you like it, research it, and if the money is right for the piece, buy it.

AC Service, Oil Filter, Fuel Pump
10½" x 18" red, white, blue & yellow painted metal,
2-sided chained & flanged sign
circa 1947–1948
$195.00 (D)

Spark Plugs Cleaned and Adjusted by the **AC**
method/5¢ Each while you wait
black & yellow rectangular metal sign
circa 1947–1948
$85.00 (D)

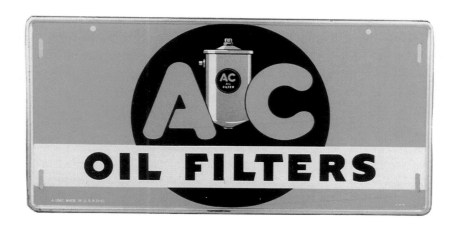

AC Oil Filters, art work of oil filter in center
18" x 8¾" yellow, black & white painted tin sign,
circa 1941; $50.00 (B)

Ace High Motor Oil *(100% Pure Pennsylvania Oil Trademark at center)*
Permit No 218 (art of scenery at center)
Midwest Oil Company, Minneapolis, Minnesota
circa 1920s; $1,250.00–$1,350.00 (C)

Jenny AERO
12" x 9"
red, white & blue porcelain pump sign
$150.00 (B)

Aetna Automobile Insurance
Aetna Insurance Company, Hartford, Connecticut
24" x 12" copper background with black lettering,
debossed painted tin; $125.00 (B)

Courtesy Gene Sonnen

ALA Emergency Service
20" x 18" red & cream,
2-sided, porcelain sign
$55.00 (D)

Alemite Pennsylvania Motor Oil
Guaranteed Uniform The Country Over
Art Deco style, Permit No.97
circa 1930s
yellow, black & red metal sign
$450.00–$550.00 (C)

Allis-Chalmers
11¼" square red, blue & white porcelain sign
$125.00 (C)

AMHA
American Motor Hotel
Association/Member 1951
20" x 15" blue, yellow, red & white,
porcelain two-sided sign
$85.00 (B)

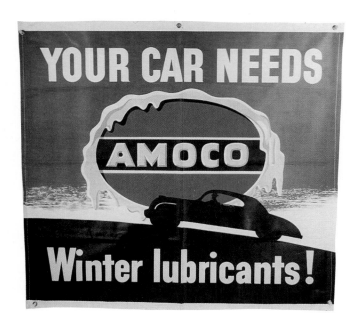

Your Car Needs **AMOCO** Winter Lubricants
art of older model car driving uphill at center-bottom
37½" x 35" light & dark blue,
red and white, cloth banner
$85.00 (B)

AMOCO *Courtesy Cards Honored Here*
American Oil Company, Troy, New York
24" x 15" red, white & black porcelain sign
$75.00 (B)

AMA, Asociacion Mexicana Automovilistica
Mexico
23" x 17½" red, white & black porcelain sign
$60.00 (B)

Armstrong Rhino-Flex *Tires*
Armstrong Tires
12" x 59" yellow & black embossed metal sign
$125.00 (B)

Courtesy Gene Sonnen

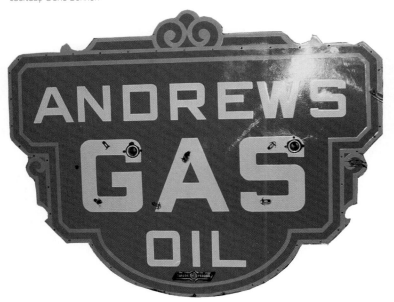

Andrews Gas/Oil
yellow, white & red neon on porcelain sign
$1,700.00–$2,100.00 (C)

Atlantic
The Atlantic Refining Company
Philadelphia, Pennsylvania
13" x 9" red, white & black pump sign
$40.00 (C)

Atlantic
The Atlantic Refining Company
Philadelphia, Pennsylvania
13" x 7" red, white & black pump sign
$40.00 (D)

Atlantic Aviation Motor Oil
Keeps Engines Clean
The Atlantic Refining Company
Philadelphia, Pennsylvania
18" x 10½" red, white & blue
painted metal sign
$75.00 (C)

Atlantic Diesel Fuel
The Atlantic Refining Company
Philadelphia, Pennsylvania
13" x 17" red, white & blue
porcelain pump sign
circa 1951; $85.00 (C)

Atlantic Gasoline *with logo in center*
The Atlantic Refining Company
Philadelphia, Pennsylvania
36" x 52" red, white & black porcelain sign
$350.00 (C)

Atlantic Imperial *shield shaped*
The Atlantic Refining Company
Philadelphia, Pennsylvania
13" x 16½" red, white, blue & gold
embossed tin sign
$55.00 (D)

Atlantic Premium
The Atlantic Refining Company
Philadelphia, Pennsylvania
13" x 11" red, white & blue porcelain pump sign
$75.00 (C)

Atlantic Refining Company
Gasoline Polarine Oils and Greases For Sale Here
The Atlantic Refining Company
Philadelphia, Pennsylvania
28" x 20" white & blue porcelain sign
$325.00 (B)

Auto-Lite Authorized Service
19" x 12½" red, yellow & black painted
metal 2-sided flanged sign
$75.00 (B)

Courtesy Gene Sonnen

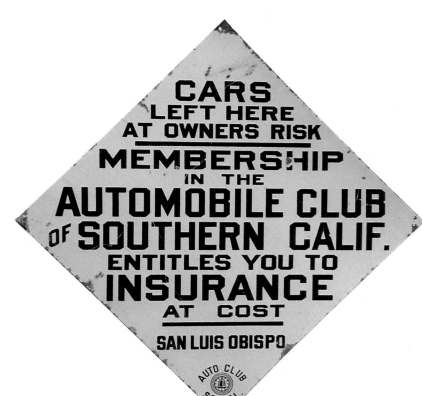

Auto-Lite Spark Plugs
Cleaning Service/Motor Tune Up
(with art of spark plug)
yellow, black, white & red
metal flange sign
$225.00 (C)

*Membership in the **Automobile Club of Southern California** entitles*
you to insurance at cost (this sign is showing some wear)
Auto Club of Southern California
San Luis Obispo, California
30" square blue & white painted metal 2-sided flanged sign
$325.00 (B)

Automotive Maintenance Association Inc.
with art of car in center and logo of the Allied
Automotive Industries at center bottom
Automotive Maintenance Association Inc.
Sacramento, California
20" x 18" embossed lettering, black & yellow
hanging porcelain sign
$300.00 (B)

Be Square/Motor Oil
(B Square logo in the center)
Barnsdall Refining Company
New York, New York
27½" diameter black, blue & cream
porcelain sign
$415.00 (B)

Courtesy Gene Sonnen

Be Square to your Motor/ The World's First Refiner/**Barnsdall**
(with art of world globe behind "B" logo)
Barnsdall Refining Company
New York, New York
blue, green, white & red metal sign
$800.00–$925.00 (C)

Battery Service *Our Batteries Last Longer Cost Less*
(Barnsdall logo at bottom right)
Barnsdall Refining Company, New York, New York
27½" x 9½" embossed lettering, black,
blue & cream painted tin sign
$75.00 (C)

Barnsdall Super-Gas
(ethyl logo at center bottom)
Barnsdall Refining Company
New York, New York
30" diameter, red, yellow & blue
porcelain 2-sided sign
$150.00 (B)

Tire Service Tube Vulcanizing
(Barnsdall logo at bottom right)
Barnsdall Refining Company
New York, New York
27½" x 9¾" black, cream & blue painted tin sign
$35.00 (C)

Accurate Information and Road Maps for Tourists
(Barnsdall logo at bottom right)
Barnsdall Refining Company, New York, New York
27½" x 10" black, cream & blue painted tin sign
$95.00 (B)

BOSTON AUTOMOBILE CLUB

Boston Automobile Club
22⅜" x 5½" red, white & blue, debossed,
porcelain hanging, two-sided sign
$150.00 (C)

Cadillac Authorized Service
(logo at center)
48" x 48"
black & white porcelain
$650.00 (B)

Carter Carburetor Service
32" x 14½" black, white &
red porcelain 2-sided sign
$125.00 (C)

Cadillac Certified Craftsman
(logo at center) J. Bendekgey
black, white, yellow &
red metal sign
$35.00 (D)

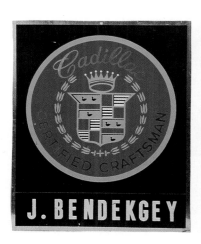

Stop at dependable garages showing this emblem
Certified Garages of America Association/To protect you
they are selected Certified Garages By Invitation
24" x 36", yellow & blue, painted tin sign
$225.00 (B)

Chalmers Motor Car Company
(logo in center)
Detroit, Michigan
20½" x 21" blue & cream metal sign
$155.00 (C)

Champlin Motor Oils *(logo in center)*
Champlin Refining Company
Enid, Oklahoma
30" diameter red, white & blue
porcelain 2-sided sign
$135.00 (C)

Champlin Gasoline
Smooth Dependable Power (logo in center)
Champlin Refining Company, Enid, Oklahoma
23.5" x 18" embossed letters, red,
white & blue tin sign
$95.00 (C)

Champlin Refining Company
Hildebrand Lease (logo at bottom left)
Champlin Refining Company
Enid, Oklahoma
26" x 10" red, white & blue
porcelain sign
$65.00 (C)

Courtesy Gene Sonnen

Champlin Hi-V-I Motor Oil
*On the ground—or in the sky
Champlin Refining Company
Enid, Oklahoma
red, black & yellow metal sign
$280.00–$400.00 (C)*

Chevrolet Service
*(logo at top center)
75¾" x 44½" red, blue, yellow,
black & white tin with wood frame
sign (showing some wear but still
a good display piece)
$190.00 (B)*

Chrysler Motor Cars
*35" x 23¾" black & white porcelain
2-sided sign (some chipping on sign)
$200.00 (C)*

Cities Service Oils Once—Always (logo in center)
Cities Service Oil Company
This company started in Tulsa, Oklahoma, as a utility
company. They then moved into the petroleum industry
as Citco in the 1960s, based in Venezuela.
10½" diameter black & white porcelain pump sign
$225.00 (B)

Citroen Sales, Service
Citroen Automobile Manufacturing
France
26" x 40½" black, yellow & white porcelain sign
(some chipping on sign but good, vivid colors)
$95.00 (D)

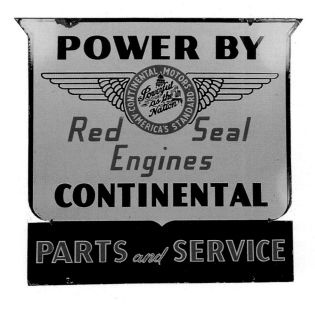

Power by Red Seal Engines,
Continental Parts and Service
(winged logo at top center)
Continental Motors
29¼" x 30¼" black, red & white porcelain sign
$285.00 (B)

Conoco Motor Oil/*A grade for each type of engine*
(featuring art of colonial minuteman)
yellow, blue, brown & white porcelain sign
$1,500.00–$2,000.00 (C)

Bonded Cooper Tires
Go As Far As You Like!
(exploded view of tire at right)
Cooper Tires
32½" x 12" embossed, blue, red
& white painted tin sign
The Scioto Sign Co. Kenton, Ohio
$225.00 (D)

Cooper Tires
(knight's helmet at top)
32½" x 12"
red, white & blue oval tin sign
$150.00 (D)

Crown Gasoline
The Standard Oil Company, Inc.
26¼" x 26" red, white & blue
flanged porcelain two-sided sign
$725.00 (C)

Courtesy Gene Sonnen

Crown Gasoline
The Standard Oil Company,
Incorporated in Kentucky
Sign marked: Ingram Richardson
Beaver Falls, Pennsylvania
24¼" x 22" red, white & blue
flanged porcelain two-sided sign
$725.00 (C)

Sunray D-X Petroleum Products
yellow, orange, red, black, green & white
porcelain pump sign
$650.00–$800.00 (C)

Sunray D-X Petroleum Products
30" diameter octagon shaped, red, orange,
yellow, white & blue porcelain sign
$800.00–$1,000.00 (C)

Courtesy Gene Sonnen

We recommend **D-X**
red, black & white porcelain double-sided sign
$165.00 (C)

Denman Handcrafted Tires
Denman Tires
58½" x 16½" embossed red, blue & light yellow metal sign
$75.00 (B)

Dunlop Tires
13¾" x 60½" black, red &
white painted metal sign
$95.00 (B)

Dodge Job-Rated Trucks Sales & Service
Dodge Trucks
42" square, yellow, blue &
white porcelain sign
$500.00 (B)

Authorized Dealer **Duplex Marine Engine Oil**
(Trade Mark) Use Kasson Waterproof Grease
Duplex Oil
20" x 10" blue, red & green painted tin sign
circa 1950; $80.00 (B)

Courtesy Gene Sonnen

Free **EN-AR-CO** Road Maps
(featuring art of boy holding U.S. map)
EN-AR-CO (The National Refining Co.)
12" x 16" black, white, red &
yellow painted tin, 2-sided sign
circa 1937; $400.00 (B)

Economy Auto/Over 2000 items for the car
(featuring art of Dallas Texas figure
sitting in a 1947 Oldsmobile)
red, black, yellow & white metal sign
$2,350.00–$2,800.00 (C)

**EN-AR-CO Motor Oil Royal Gasoline/
White Rose Gasoline**
(featuring art of boy holding chalkboard)
EN-AR-CO (The National Refining Co.)
red, black, yellow & white small tin sign
$1,925.00–$2,400.00 (C)

Courtesy Gene Sonnen

EN-AR-CO Motor Oil/White Rose Gasoline
(featuring art of boy holding chalkboard)
EN-AR-CO (The National Refining Co.)
red, black, yellow & white large
3-piece porcelain sign
$1,925.00–$2,400.00 (C)

Edison Pep! Spark Plugs
(featuring art of racing spark plug engine with wheels)
31" tall, four-color cardboard stand-up advertisement sign
circa 1934
$825.00–$950.00 (C)

Courtesy Gene Sonnen

Esso Tiger/Put a Tiger in Your Tank!
Standard Oil Company
New Jersey
42" x 83" yellow, black, orange & white plastic banner
$185.00 (D)

Esso Credit Cards Honored
Standard Oil Company
New Jersey
18" x 14" blue, white & red porcelain, 2-sided sign
$80.00 (B)

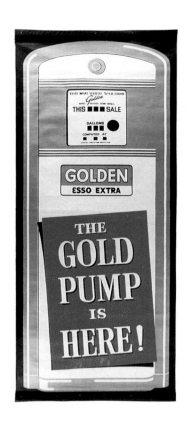

When It's an **Exide** You Start
(picture of battery in center
and touring car at lower left)
Exide
11¾" x 15" black, red, &
white painted metal sign
$150.00 (B)

Golden Esso Extra, The Gold Pump Is Here (picture of gold pump)
(The Standard Oil Company started using the Esso Brand in 1926,
and that was replaced by Exxon brand in 1972.)
New Jersey
36" x 83" canvas banner
$75.00–$100.00 (C)

*Garage/**Firestone** tires/gasoline*
Firestone
Akron, Ohio
(Founded in Akron in 1900, this company
produced the first solid rubber tires in
1903. Then in the early 1930s Firestone
made a practical air filled tire.)
21" x 16" blue, orange & white
porcelain, flanged sign
$275.00 (D)

Fisk Tires
*yellow, blue & white porcelain,
flanged sign
$450.00–$600.00 (C)*

Ford
*70" x 35½"
blue & white oval light-up sign
$1,450.00 (B)*

Francisco Auto Heater/*Summer Here all the Year*
*(Winter scene with cut-away car showing Francisco Auto Heater)
40" x 18" self-contained framed tin sign
$725.00 (B)*

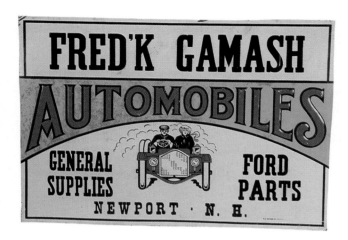

Fred'k Gamash Automobiles
General Supplies/Ford parts
Newport, New Hampshire
19¾" x 13⅝" black, red, yellow &
white metal sign
$145.00 (B)

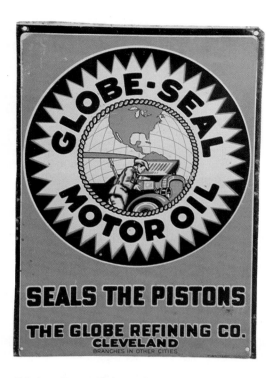

Globe-Seal Motor Oil *seal the pistons*
(globe with mechanic filling auto with oil)
The Globe Refining Co.
Cleveland, Ohio/with branches in other cities
9½" x 14" blue, orange & white painted tin sign
$275.00 (B)

Courtesy Gene Sonnen

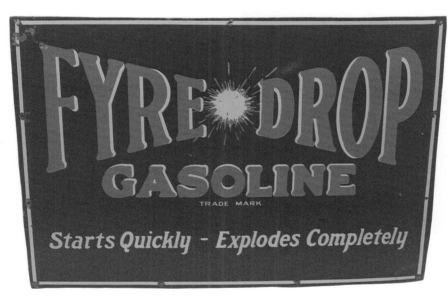

Fyre Drop Gasoline/*Starts Quickly — Explodes Completely*
yellow, red & black porcelain sign
$700.00–$875.00 (C)

Golden Tip Gasoline
Louisville, Kentucky
48" long arrow shape metal sign
$450.00–$800.00 (C)

B. F. Goodrich/*1870*
(tire artwork in center of sign)
B. F. Goodrich
Akron, Ohio
35" x 23" black, red, yellow &
white painted tin sign
Made in U. S. A. MCA-249 Property of the B. F.
Goodrich Co Akron, Ohio. Stock No 8-390-EG at
the top edge
$110.00 (B)

Goodrich, *Jno. A Hastings/Paullina,*
Iowa/Goodrich/Black safety tread tires
(picture of older model tire mounted on spoke wheel)
B. F. Goodrich, Akron, Ohio
37¾" x 11½" black, red, & white, embossed painted tin sign
$350.00 (B)

Goodrich Silvertones
B. F. Goodrich, Akron, Ohio
23" x 19" blue & white, debossed,
porcelain, flanged, two-sided sign
$300.00 (B)

Air Service Goodrich Tires
11" x 9" red & yellow porcelain two-sided sign
$135.00 (D)

Goodrich Tires • Batteries
B. F. Goodrich, Akron, Ohio
72" x 17" blue & white, porcelain sign
$125.00 (D)

You'll get more and quicker heat with this
Goodrich *Hot Water Heater*
heat condition your car this winter
(art of heater at right)
57" x 34" cream, black, orange,
red & yellow paper sign
M C A Sign Co. Massillon, Ohio
$45.00 (D)

*Blue Garage/Stamford, N.Y./****Goodyear***
tires/storage supplies, etc.
Goodyear
Akron, Ohio
36" x 11¾" black, red & white, painted
metal sign with some overall rust
$60.00 (B)

Goodyear *Service Station/R. G. Cross, LaGrangeville - N. Y. (picture of tire at left) Goodyear Akron, Ohio 21¾" x 12" black, red & white, painted tin flanged sign $135.00 (D)*

Goodyear Tires *(winged foot logo at center & Goodyear flag at center top) Goodyear, Akron, Ohio 53¼" x 30½" yellow, blue & white, porcelain two-sided sign $95.00 (D)*

Gulf No-Nox Motor Fuel
*Gulf Refining Company
Boston/New York/
Philadelphia/Houston/Atlanta/
New Orleans/ Louisville
18¼" x 18" orange, light & dark blue,
& white porcelain flanged sign
$200.00 (B)*

Gulf Supreme *motor oil, At the sign of the orange disc (picture of older touring car at bottom) Even though this sign is not in the best of shape, it still held its own at auction. Gulf Refining Company Boston/New York/Philadelphia/Houston/Atlanta/ New Orleans/ Louisville 27½" x 60" orange, light & dark blue, & white porcelain sign $440.00 (B)*

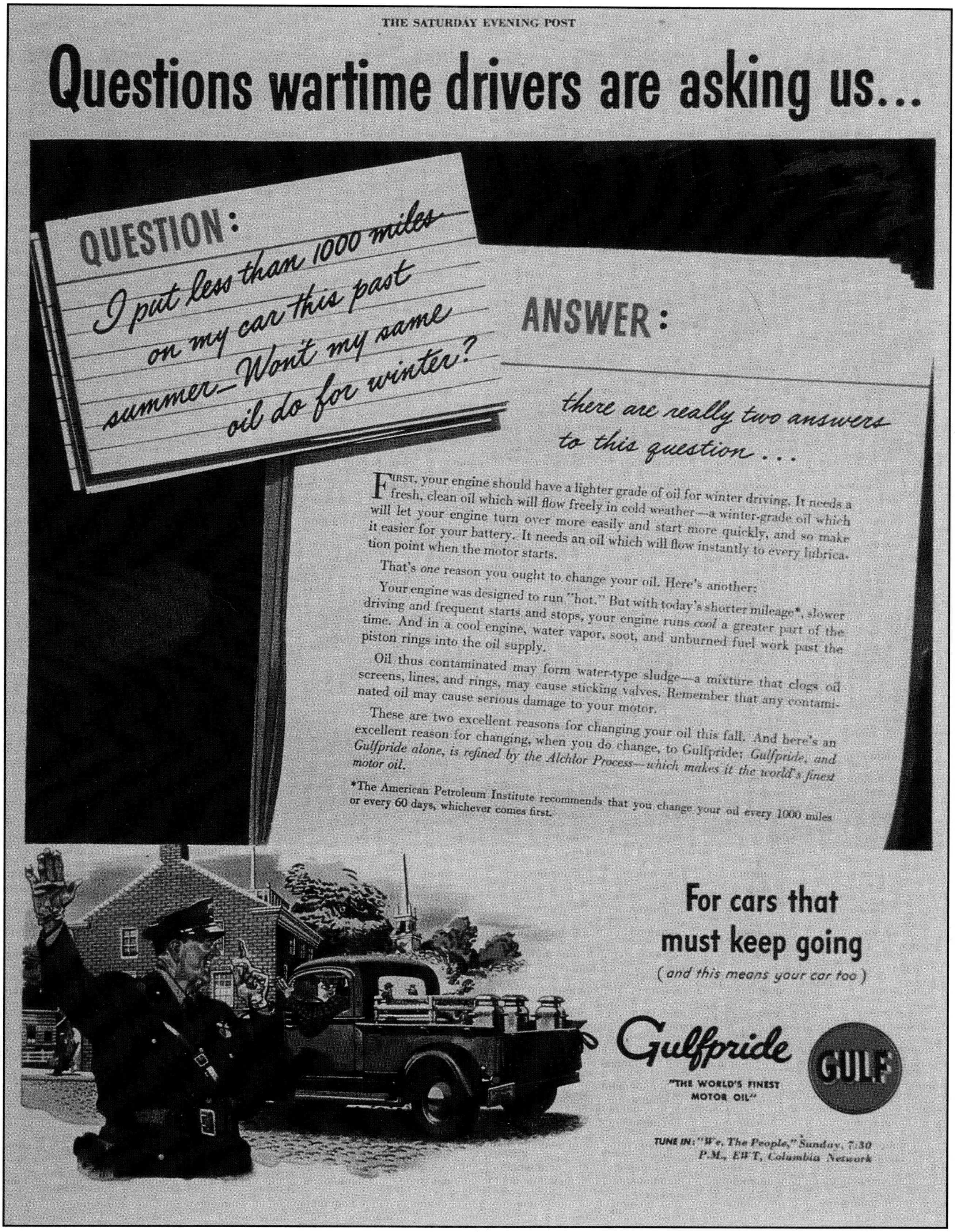

Questions wartime drivers are asking us...

QUESTION: I put less than 1000 miles on my car this past summer—Won't my same oil do for winter?

ANSWER:

there are really two answers to this question...

First, your engine should have a lighter grade of oil for winter driving. It needs a fresh, clean oil which will flow freely in cold weather—a winter-grade oil which will let your engine turn over more easily and start more quickly, and so make it easier for your battery. It needs an oil which will flow instantly to every lubrication point when the motor starts.

That's *one* reason you ought to change your oil. Here's another:

Your engine was designed to run "hot." But with today's shorter mileage*, slower driving and frequent starts and stops, your engine runs *cool* a greater part of the time. And in a cool engine, water vapor, soot, and unburned fuel work past the piston rings into the oil supply.

Oil thus contaminated may form water-type sludge—a mixture that clogs oil screens, lines, and rings, may cause sticking valves. Remember that any contaminated oil may cause serious damage to your motor.

These are two excellent reasons for changing your oil this fall. And here's an excellent reason for changing, when you do change, to Gulfpride: Gulfpride, and Gulfpride alone, is refined by the Alchlor Process—which makes it the world's finest motor oil.

*The American Petroleum Institute recommends that you change your oil every 1000 miles or every 60 days, whichever comes first.

For cars that must keep going

(and this means your car too)

Gulfpride

"THE WORLD'S FINEST MOTOR OIL"

GULF

TUNE IN: "We, The People," Sunday, 7:30 P.M., EWT, Columbia Network

Gulf light-up sign
Gulf Refining Company
27" diameter x 7" deep orange, blue, &
white metal-framed plastic light-up sign
1981 date on bottom center
$275.00 (D)

Courtesy Gene Sonnen

Gulf Authorized Dealer
dark blue & white porcelain sign
$400.00–$500.00 (C)

Courtesy Gene Sonnen

Harbor Petroleum Products
(featuring art of airplane landing on water at top)
light blue, orange, yellow, black & white porcelain sign
$4,400.00 (B)

Hastings *Free Compression Test Station/Piston rings (Detective Hastings in center) 19½" x 27½" red, black & white painted tin sign $85.00 (B)*

Hood Tire *Dealer red, black & white cut out man in uniform $3,000.00–$4,750.00 (C)*

Courtesy Gene Sonnen

Courtesy Gene Sonnen

Hood Tire *Dealer red, black & white small porcelain die cut man in uniform $2,500.00–$3,000.00 (C)*

Hood Tires *Authorized Hood Dealer red, black, & yellow tin sign $1,325.00–$1,600.00 (C)*

Hudson Sales Service Rambler
42" x 30" red, black & white, porcelain
two-sided sign
$500.00 (C)

For Your Safety We Don't Smoke On Driveway
(art of **Humble** service station attendant at left)
Humble (Standard Oil purchased Humble in
1919), Huston, Texas
14" x 10" green & white porcelain sign
$425.00 (B)

Courtesy of Gene Sonnen

Husky Service
(with art of husky dog at top)
red, black, white & yellow porcelain sign
$1,200.00–$1,600.00 (C)

Hyvis Motor Oil
Super-refined pure Pennsylvania/Permit No. 4
27¾" x 16¾" red, blue, yellow & white tin sign
$155.00 (D)

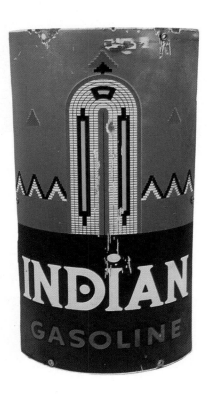

Independent Gasoline
(with Ethyl logo in center)
30" diameter, red, blue, black, white &
yellow, porcelain sign
$225.00–$250.00 (C)

Indian Gasoline
(with Indian design at top)
Indian Refining Company
New York, New York, circa 1940
18" tall rounded, red, yellow, blue, green & white porcelain pump sign
$175.00–$225.00 (C)

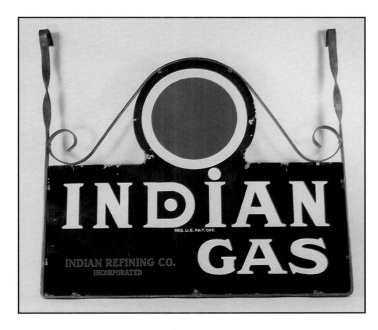

Indian Gas
Indian Refining Co. Incorporated
45" x 36" red, blue & white wrought iron framed porcelain two-sided sign
$500.00 (B)

Courtesy of Gene Sonnen

Indian Gasoline *with art of Indians at right and left*
Indian Refining Co. Incorporated
red, black & white tin sign (very old and very rare)
$1,300.00–$1,600.00 (C)

Information Free/Touring Bureau Official Station
16" x 16", blue & white embossed porcelain, two-sided sign
$70.00 (D)

Johnson Time Tells Motor Oil
(art of hourglass with wings)
48" diameter blue, orange & white
embossed porcelain, two-sided sign
$600.00–$800.00 (C)

Courtesy of Gene Sonnen

Johnson Brilliant Bronze
(art of hourglass with wings)
orange, black & white porcelain pump sign
$500.00–$650.00 (C)

Kendall the 2000 mile oil
(art of older model plane, car and bus)
red, black & white sign
$500.00–$700.00 (C)

Penzbest Kendall Motor Oils
(100% Pure Pennsylvania Oil)
36" diameter red white & blue
porcelain sign
$375.00–$650.00 (C)

H. E. King *Automotive Painting*
70¾" x 19" gold & black wood
framed sign
$55.00 (D)

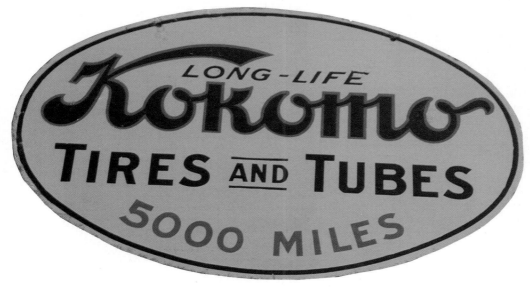

Long-Life **Kokomo** *Tires and Tubes, 5000 Miles*
Oval red, yellow & black sign
$300.00–$475.00 (C)

The Perfect **Koolmotor**, *A Cities Service*
Product, Pennsylvania Oil with a rare Cities
Service sign base
green, black, white & red lollipop
2 sided porcelain sign
$525.00–$600.00 (C)

Courtesy of Gene Sonnen

The Perfect **Koolmotor**,
A Cities Service Product Penna. Oil
Cities Service Oil Company
24" diameter, green, red, black &
white porcelain 2-sided sign
$350.00 (B)

Refill with **Koolmotor** The Perfect Pennsylvania Oil
Cities Service Oil Company
green, black, red & white porcelain sign
$400.00–$500.00 (C)

Courtesy of Gene Sonnen

Koolmotor Bronze Gasoline
Cities Service Oil Company
yellow, black, red & white banner
$500.00–$675.00 (C)

Courtesy of Gene Sonnen

Gold Medal Auto Oil/The **Kunz Oil**
(globe art at left)
Kunz Oil Oil Company
Minneapolis-St. Paul
yellow, black & red tin sign
$415.00–$525.00 (C)

Linco Gasoline *with art of runner*
yellow, black & red rare porcelain sign
Linco was bought out by Marathon
$875.00–$1,000.00 (C)

Courtesy of Gene Sonnen

Linco Gasoline Oils
24" diameter red, white & black porcelain
two-sided sign
$390.00–$500.00 (C)

We Fit **Lodge** Spark Plugs
(picture of spark plug at left)
18" x 12" red, yellow, & black painted tin sign
$60.00 (B)

Magnolene Motor Oil for Fords Reduces Vibration
Magnolia Oil Co.
Socony purchased Magnolia in 1918. And was
eventually purchased by Standard Oil Company
22" x 16" blue & white , porcelain 2 –sided sign
$450.00 (B)

Magnolia Gasoline/Motor Oil
(with Magnolia flower art)
Magnolia Oil Co
42" diameter, blue, red, yellow, green
& white, porcelain 2-sided sign
$300.00–$375.00 (B)

*Magnolia Petroleum Company/Magnolene Motor Oils for sale here
(with Magnolia flower art at top center)
Magnolia Oil Co
round, blue, red, yellow, green
& white, porcelain sign
$385.00–$600.00 (C)*

*Magnolia Petroleum Company/
Magnolia Gasoline for sale here
(with Magnolia flower art at top center)
Magnolia Oil Co
round, blue, red, yellow, green
& white, porcelain sign
$385.00–$600.00 (C)*

*Magnolia Gasoline
(with Ethyl trademark at center)
Magnolia Oil Co
round, blue, red, yellow, & white,
porcelain sign
$385.00–$600.00 (C)*

Marland Gasoline*/look for the red triangle*
(red triangle logo at left)
Marland Oils
(This company bought Continental Oil Company in the late 1920s, but decided
to use the Continental name. Later they became Conoco Oil Company.)
29" x 14", red, yellow & black, embossed painted tin sign
$125.00 (D)

Marathon *Products Best In the Long Run with*
art of marathon runner
teal, gold, black & white round metal sign
$675.00 (C)

Marathon Motor Oils*/Best in the Long Run*
(featuring art of older model car and marathon runner)
Transcontinental Oil Company
New York City • Sioux City, Iowa • Des Moines, Iowa • Pittsburg, Pennsylvania
rectangular orange, lime, dark green & white metal sign
$1,350.00 (C)

Marathon Ethyl
(featuring Ethyl logo and marathon runner)
Transcontinental Oil Company
*New York City • Sioux City, Iowa • Des
Moines, Iowa • Pittsburgh, Pennsylvania
round, green, yellow, black & white metal sign
$675.00–$1,000.00 (C)*

Courtesy of Gene Sonnen

Marvel *Non-Liquid Battery*
*red, yellow & black flange tin sign
$225.00–$300.00 (C)*

Midwest Gasoline and Motor Oils
*round red, blue & white porcelain sign
$375.00 (D)*

Miller Tires/Geared-to-the-road
73¼" x 21¾", yellow, white &
black, wood framed porcelain sign
$125.00 (D)

Courtesy of Gene Sonnen

Mobiloil (gargoyle logo at top)
Vacuum Oil Company
red, white & black embossed tin sign
$225.00–$300.00 (C)

Mobiloil Gargoyle Certified Service
19½" X 19½" black, red & white porcelain sign
$425.00 (C)

Mobiloil (oil can artwork with Pegasus)
Socony-Vacuum Oil Company Inc.
made in U. S. A.
29" x 39", red, white, blue & black, cloth banner
$125.00–$175.00 (C)

Mobiloil
(art work of Pegasus at center top)
12" x 12", red, white, & blue,
die cut porcelain pump sign
circa 1946; $350.00 (B)

Mobilfuel/diesel
(art work of Pegasus at center top)
12" x 12", red, white, & blue, die
cut porcelain pump sign
$275.00 (B)

Mobiloil/Marine (artwork of Pegasus at center top)
(As a rule, marine signs bring a good price due in part to their
scarcity and the fact that there are collectors that specialize in
only marine collectibles.)
31" diameter, red, white, & blue, porcelain curb two-sided sign
$650.00 (B)

Mobil/Marine white
red, white, & blue, porcelain pump sign
$150.00 (B)

Mobil/Upperlube/Extra protection for your engine
(Socony-Vacuum logo at center bottom)
Socony-Vacuum Oil Company Inc.
made in U. S. A.
16" x 8¾" red, white & blue, light-up display tin
frame with glass front sign
$325.00 (B)

Mobilgas Special (red Pegasus at top)
12" x 12" red, white & blue ,die-cut porcelain sign
circa 1947
$145.00 (D)

Courtesy of Gene Sonnen

Mobilgas with Pegasus at top
red, white & blue shield shaped pump sign
$110.00–$165.00 (C)

Courtesy of Gene Sonnen

Mobilgas Marine with Pegasus at top
red, white & blue shield shaped pump sign
$900.00–$1,100.00 (C)

Mobilgas Ethyl (Ethyl trademark at top)
30" diameter red, white, yellow & black,
porcelain sign
$375.00–$450.00 (C)

Mohawk Tires
58½" x 16¾" yellow & green, painted tin sign
$75.00 (B)

Monogram *Oils And Greases*
(Balto Enl & Nob. Co., M. D., 490 W B-way NY)
at lower right corner of sign
18" x 3" red & white, porcelain flanged sign
$350.00 (B)

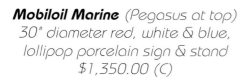

Mobiloil Marine *(Pegasus at top)*
30" diameter red, white & blue,
lollipop porcelain sign & stand
$1,350.00 (C)

Expert Car Washing A Careful High Grade Inspected Job!
*(Authorized **Mona-Motor** Service System)*
Monarch Manufacturing Co., Council Bluffs, Iowa
(This company and Barnsdall merged in the late 1920s)
27½" x 9¾" embossed lettering black, blue & cream painted tin sign
$65.00 (D)

Monogram Greases and Oils
24" x 15" black, red & white, porcelain
flanged two-sided sign
$375.00 (B)

Authorized Nash Service
42" x 42" light & dark green two-sided porcelain sign
$480.00 (B)

National Batteries (eagle art in center)
20" x 12" orange & black, painted tin sign
$150.00 (B)

Authorized Niehoff Automotive Products Distributor
11¼" diameter red & black on white,
gold metal rim, glass face, light-up sign
$95.00 (C)

Noco Motor Oil/Strictly Pennsylvania
Northwestern Oil Company
Superior, Wisconsin/Rhinelander, Wisconsin/St. Cloud Minnesota/St. Paul Minnesota/
Port Arthur, Ontario/Bemidji, Minnesota/Duluth, Minnesota
yellow, white & black embossed tin picture sign
$1,495.00 (C)

Smoking/Carrying Matches/Open Lights/
Positively Prohibited
no company
28" x 20", red & white porcelain sign
$40.00 (B)

Gasoline and Oil
no company
36" x 24", yellow & black,
wood framed tin, two-sided sign
$350.00 (B)

NO AUTOS FILLED
WHILE ENGINES RUNNING
OIL OR GAS LIGHTS BURNING
OR OCCUPANTS SMOKING

*No Autos Filled While Engines Running Oil
or Gas Lights Burning or Occupants Smoking
no company
18" x 12", red & white, porcelain sign
$235.00 (B)*

NOTICE
FILLING SERVICE
WILL NOT BE RENDERED
WHILE MOTORS ARE RUNNING,
OCCUPANTS SMOKING
OR LAMPS BURNING.

*Notice filling service will not be rendered while motors
are running, occupants smoking, or lamps burning
no company
22" x 18", red, green & white, porcelain sign
$150.00 (B)*

*Danger/No Smoking Matches or Open Lights
no company
14½" x 10½", red & white, porcelain sign
$55.00 (C)*

*Tire & Battery Service
no company
42" x 7", red & white, painted metal, two-sided sign
$75.00 (B)*

Curb-Service
no company
24" x 6", green & white, porcelain sign
$125.00 (D)

Dealer
no company
41" x 8", red & white, porcelain, two-sided sign
circa 1934; $100.00 (D)

Crankcase-Service
no company
40" x 10", orange, blue & white,
porcelain sign
$95.00 (B)

Quick Service/All Makes of Cars
no company
sign produced by C-I-Brink South Boston, Mass
53½" x 30", blue & white, porcelain sign
$125.00 (C)

Service Entrance
no company
42¼" x 10", blue & white, arrow
shaped, porcelain sign
$200.00 (B)

*For Use As A Motor Fuel Only/
Contains Lead (Tetra ethyl)
no company
7" x 6", black & white, porcelain pump sign
$35.00 (B)*

*All Traffic Stop Order of Police
no company
22" x 22", black & yellow, octagon
shaped wooden sign with reflectors
$150.00 (D)*

*Barter's Garage Tenants harbor auto
electric service/**Oilzum** America's finest
oil (Oilzum man in "O" of Oilzum)
The White Bagley Co.
Worchester, Massachusetts
60" x 36", black, orange &
white wood-framed tin sign
$1,700.00 (B)*

***Olixir** sealed protection/The modern lubrication aid
16" x 8¾" black, red, & yellow two-sided tin sign
$75.00–$100.00 (C)*

Overland Service
Hageman & Kretsinger, Leaf River
23½" x 12", orange & black,
embossed letter, painted tin sign
$150.00 (B)

Stop at **Overland** *Col. Garage, Keene*
(Early automobile in top left corner)
25" x 13", orange & black,
wood-framed, tin sign
$200.00 (B)

Approved **Packard** *Service*
41.75" diameter, red, white & blue, porcelain sign
(slightly retouched)
$500.00–$600.00 (C)

Courtesy of Gene Sonnen

Pankey *Oils/Nothing Better*
(art of early tanker truck)
red, white & black tin picture sign
$1,395.00 (C)

Courtesy of Gene Sonnen

Paragon Gasolene
(with art of early tanker truck, oil derrick, and refinery)
red, white, green & black porcelain lollipop sign
(The rarity of this sign is determined by the word
"gasolene." Most have Paragon Motor Oil.)
$5,500.00 (C)

*Authorized Distributor **Penndurol***
(100% Pure Pennsylvania Oil trademark at top center)
48" x 36" yellow, white & blue, porcelain sign
$375.00–$500.00 (C)

Pennfield Motor Oil
(derrick art behind Pennfield)
(100% Pure Pennsylvania Oil trademark
at top left)
round, red, white & black,
self-framed porcelain sign
$575.00 (B)

Penno Unexcelled Motor Oil, Permit No 49
(100% Pure Pennsylvania Oil trademark at bottom center)
rectangular, red, white & black, two-sided porcelain sign
$350.00–$550.00 (C)

Courtesy of Gene Sonnen

Penno Unexcelled Drain and Refill Now
(100% Pure Pennsylvania Oil trademark at bottom center)
rectangular, red, white & black, porcelain sign
sold by W. H. Barber, Makers of Fyre Drop Gasolene and Meteeor
$425.00–$500.00 (C)

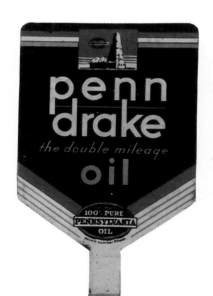

Penn-Drake the double mileage oil
(featuring picture of Drake oilwell at top center)
Pennsylvania Refining Company
Butler, Pennsylvania
(This company was purchased by Pennzoil in the 1970s.)
5" x 6½", red, blue & white painted metal two-sided sign
$55.00 (B)

Guaranteed 100% Pure Pennsylvania Oil
(trademark) Permit No. 1
12" x 9¾" yellow & black,
die-cut porcelain pump sign
$130.00 (B)

Pennsylvania Tires
15" x 59¾", red, white & black, painted metal sign
$70.00 (B)

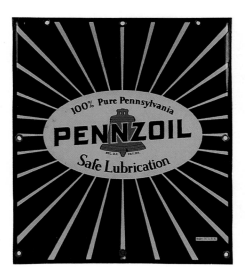

*100% Pure **Pennsylvania Pennzoil** Safe Lubrication (logo in center)*
Pennzoil, Oil City, Pennsylvania & Houston, Texas
(In the 1920s and 1930s Pennzoil gasoline changed their brand to
Pennzip and also sold "Transport" brand gasoline.)
13" x 15", red, black & yellow porcelain pump sign
$325.00 (B)

Phillips 66 *(Ethyl logo in center)*
Phillips Petroleum Company
Bartlesville, Oklahoma
(Phillips was founded in 1917
by Frank Phillips & friends.)
30" diameter, yellow, white & black,
porcelain two-sided sign
$350.00 (B)

Pennsylvania Motor Federation *with triple "A" in center*
Automobile Club of Pittsburgh, Pennsylvania
3½" diameter, red, green, black & white
porcelain license plate attachment
$75.00 (C)

Phillips 66 (Shield Shaped Sign)
Phillips Petroleum Company
Bartlesville, Oklahoma; circa 1954
48" x 48" orange & black,
embossed porcelain sign
$500.00–$700.00 (C)

Phillips 66 (Shield) Motor Oil 100% Paraffin Base
Phillips Petroleum Company
Bartlesville, Oklahoma
24" diameter orange, white & black,
embossed porcelain sign
$450.00–$700.00 (C)

Courtesy of Gene Sonnen

Phillips 66 (Shield) Ethyl logo in starburst at center
Phillips Petroleum Company, Bartlesville, Oklahoma
yellow, orange, white & black, shield shaped porcelain sign
Ethyl logo has Ethyl Gasoline Corporation New York, U. S. A. in bottom banner
$1,800.00–$2,200.00 (C)

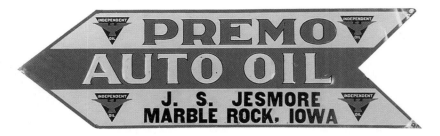

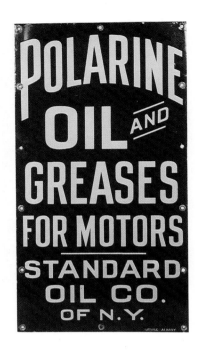

Premo *Auto Oil (Independent logo in all 4 corners)*
J. S. Jesmore, Marble Rock, Iowa
36" x 11", red, black & white painted die-cut tin sign
$145.00 (B)

Courtesy of Gene Sonnen

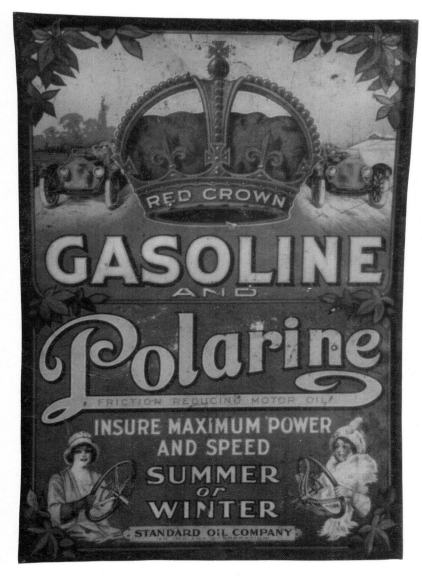

Polarine *Oil and Greases for motors*
Standard Oil Co. of New York
12" x 22", dark green & white
porcelain two-sided sign
flip side of sign has "Keep Off Sidewalk"
$275.00 (D)

Red Crown *Gasoline/***Polarine**
Standard Oil Co.
four-color art, cardboard sign
Very old and in excellent condition
$4,100.00 (B)

Power-lube Motor Oil/Smooth as the Tread of a Tiger
(featuring tiger art and 100% Pure Pennsylvania Oil logo)
Powerine Company
sign produced by: Wolverine Porcelain, Detroit/this is
property of the Powerine Co.
28" x 20", yellow, white & black, porcelain two-sided sign
$935.00 (B)

The Pure Oil Company
U. S. A./Purol Pep
The Pure Oil Company U. S. A.
15" diameter, red, white & blue,
porcelain sign; $425.00 (B)

Purolator
7" x 30" red & white,
porcelain pole sign
$65.00 (D)

Pure Premium/Be Sure With Pure
The Pure Oil Company U. S. A.
10" x 12" red, white & blue,
porcelain pump sign
$55.00 (C)

Tiolene Motor Oil (*Pure Oil logo at right*)
The Pure Oil Company U. S. A.
70" x 18" white & blue, porcelain sign
$135.00 (B)

Puritan Motor Oil (*Policeman art at left*)
The Pure Oil Company U. S. A.
35" x 11⅛" yellow & black, painted tin sign
$325.00 (B)

Courtesy of Gene Sonnen

Puritan Gasoline and Motor Oils/*the sign of the Cop (cop art at right)*
rectangular red, white & black, flange porcelain sign
$1,500.00–$1,695.00 (C)

Drain and refill with **Tiolene Motor Oil**
The Pure Oil Company U. S. A.
34" x 43" blue & white, porcelain sign
$160.00 (B)

Automobile **Peugeot**
Peugeot
38½" x 19" yellow & black, porcelain sign
$55.00 (D)

Use **Quaker State** Cold Test Oil for Winter Driving
Quaker State Motor Oil Company
St. Louis, Missouri
26½" x 6" green & white, porcelain sign
$150.00 (D)

Quaker State Motor Oil Certified Guaranteed
(Quaker State logo in center)
Quaker State Motor Oil Company
St. Louis, Missouri
(Paraland gasoline was also sold by this company
in the 1930s.)
26½" x 29" green & white, porcelain sign
$125.00–$175.00 (C)

None but the finest ... with a Vengeance!

WHEN the pilot of this Vultee Vengeance goes upstairs, he's invading disputed territory—*hotly* disputed by Messerschmitts, Focke-Wulfs and hornet-y little Zeros. Naturally, he wants to be sure that everything about his ship is in perfect condition; the motor most of all. It must keep turning over. The success of his mission—his very life—depends on it.

All over the world in this war there are Allied fighting men whose lives depend on their motors. These vital motors need oil that will keep right on providing essential lubrication, in the longest pulls and in the hottest spots.

It is our good fortune that our planes enjoy the advantage of such oils. Neither by plunder nor by discovery in synthetics has the Axis been able to provide anything to equal the quality of these oils.

For there is only one place in all the world where the *best* crude oil is found—the Pennsylvania oil field. And, in Quaker State's four great modern refineries this oil is processed with skill and care to make the finest oils that money can buy—oils with that "Pennsylvania Plus."

In these war days especially, you'll find it pays to give the motor in your car the finest protective lubrication. Infrequent driving increases rather than lessens the need for such care. So drive in for Quaker State Motor Oil and Quaker State Superfine Lubricants wherever you see the green-and-white Quaker State service sign—Quaker State Oil Refining Corporation, Oil City, Pennsylvania.

QUAKER STATE MOTOR OIL
CERTIFIED and GUARANTEED

Retail price 35¢ per quart

OIL IS AMMUNITION—USE IT WISELY

Quincy Gasoline/*from Coast to Coast/Independent Oil*
(stylized eagle in center)
Independent Oil
48" diameter, black, red & white, cast iron framed, porcelain two-sided sign
$275.00 (B)

Rajah Motor Oil
with Rajah figure head at top
Minneapolis, Minnesota
rectangular red, white & black, flanged tin sign
(only one picture globe of this company is know to exist and it is damaged!)
$1,200.00–$1,400.00 (C)

Red Crown Gasoline
Standard Oil Company of Nebraska
(Standard Oil Company of Nebraska merged with Standard Oil of Indiana in the 1940s)
rectangular red, white, blue and gold porcelain sign
fairly rare
$750.00–$950.00 (C)

Courtesy of Gene Sonnen

Red Crown Gasoline
(red crown art in center)
Standard Oil Company
42" diameter, red, white & blue,
porcelain, two-sided sign
$800.00 (B)

Red Indian Motor Oils
orange, red, white & black, porcelain oil rack sign
(mint and rare)
$825.00–$975.00 (C)

Red Giant Oils Sold Here
red & white, embossed tin sign
(mint and rare)
$125.00 (C)

Courtesy of Gene Sonnen

Authorized Service **Republic Motor Truck**
Republic
48" x 27" red, white, black,
yellow & green, porcelain sign
$375.00 (B)

Cars & Trucks All Makes/(R & G in center)
Renewed/Guaranteed
Sales Equipment Co.; Detroit, Michigan
56¾" x 29", red, blue & white porcelain sign
$95.00 (C)

Royaline Gasoline Pennsylvania Motor
Oils Hi-Test (R&C with tire in center art)
30" diameter, white, black & blue,
porcelain two-sided sign
$1,400.00 (B)

Stop Your Motor/No Smoking (**Seaside** logo in center)
Seaside
36" x 6", red, blue & cream, porcelain two-sided sign
$650.00 (B)

Here Soon, **Richfield** the Gasoline of Power
(art of close up of goggled driver, older model car, and
Richfield logo shield)
39½" x 54½" red, orange, black, yellow & green, poster
$175.00 (B)

Seiberling Tires *(Seiberling logo at bottom)*
30" x 16", orange, blue & white, porcelain two-sided sign
$200.00 (B)

Seiberling Tires
18" x 72", yellow & brown, embossed tin sign
$100.00 (B)

Shamrock Cloud Master Premium
(shamrock shape at top center)
10½" x 12½", dark & light blue and
white, porcelain pump sign
$130.00 (B)

Shell/*No Smoking, No Matches, No Naked Lights*
(Shell logo at top)
Shell Oil Company; Houston, Texas
18" x 12", red & white, porcelain sign
$125.00 (D)

Shell clam logo
Shell Oil Company
Houston, Texas
bottom right corner of above sign

Shell clam logo
Shell Oil Company; Houston, Texas
40", red & yellow, shell-shaped porcelain sign
$600.00–$800.00 (C)

Shell clam logo
Shell Oil Company
Houston, Texas
24", red & yellow, shell-shaped porcelain sign
$450.00–$850.00 (C)

Courtesy of Gene Sonnen

Shell *clam logo*
Shell Oil Company; Houston, Texas
48, red & yellow, shell-shaped porcelain sign
$500.00–$900.00 (C)

Shell-Penn *Motor Oil*
black, red & yellow, clam shaped tin sign
$875.00–$975.00 (C)

Courtesy of Gene Sonnen

Notice Smoking is Absolutely Prohibited...
Shell Petroleum Corporation
red & yellow, porcelain sign
$250.00–$325.00 (C)

Shellubrication
*Certified and Guaranteed Lubrication Service
Shell Petroleum Corporation
red, orange, black & yellow, porcelain sign
$500.00–$700.00 (C)*

Courtesy of Gene Sonnen

Shell Gas *station/Chevrolet Dealership/Ford
Automobile photograph
Shell Oil Company
20½" x 16½", early sepia framed photograph
$75.00 (B)*

Sinclair/*We Give The Best Service In Town!
Sinclair Oil Company; New York, New York
large clear background window sign
$45.00 (C)*

SINCLAIR

Sinclair
Sinclair Oil Company
New York, New York
red, green & black, porcelain sign (taken off a tanker truck)
circa 1930s; $450.00–$650.00 (C)

Sinclair Opaline Motor Oil
(picture of oil container at left)
Sinclair Oil Company (founded in 1916)
New York, New York
19½" x 12", cream, red & green tin sign
$160.00 (B)

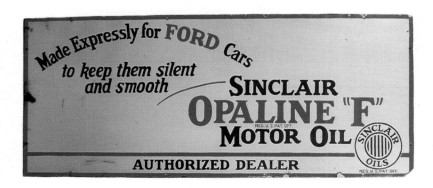

Sinclair Opaline "F" Motor Oil/Made Expressly for Ford
Cars (Sinclair Oils logo at bottom right) Authorized Dealer
Sinclair Oil Company; New York, New York
47¾" x 20", white, red & green porcelain sign
$375.00 (B)

Sinclair Oils logo
Sinclair Oil Company
New York, New York
round, white & green porcelain
pump sign
$400.00 (B)

Sinclair Aircraft *with art of airplane in center*
Sinclair Oil Company
New York, New York
round, red, white & green porcelain sign
$2,000.00–$3,000.00 (C)

Top Quality Iso/Vis "D" Motor Oil
(This shortened name comes from Indiana Standard Oil Company/Viscosity)
Indiana Standard Oil Company
Pat # 1951325
15¾" x 60¼", red, white & blue porcelain sign
$325.00 (C)

Standard Motor Gasoline*/Polarine Oil*
Standard Oil Co.
30" diameter, red, white & blue,
two-sided porcelain sign
$195.00 (D)

100% Pure Paraffin Base RPM Motor Oil
Standard Oil Co.
28" diameter, red, white & black, two-sided porcelain sign
$275.00 (B)

Money can't buy a better oil than The New Zerolene
(Zerolene logo at bottom center)
Standard Oil Company
27" x 27", white & blue, porcelain sign
$100.00 (B)

Motor Oils & Lubricants **RPM** (Chevron at center bottom)
Standard Oil Company
26" diameter, cream, red & blue, painted tin two-sided sign
$65.00 (D)

We Sell **Standard Motor Oil**/Makes Motors Run Smoother and Costs Run Lower
(Standard logo at left)
Standard Oil Company
36" x 18", white, red & blue, porcelain sign
$750.00 (B)

Socony-Vacuum/Every 1000 Miles (art of car with man driving
& woman passenger and Socony-Vacuum logo at bottom)
Socony-Vacuum Oil Company Inc.
made in U. S. A.
29" x 39" red, orange, green, white & blue, cloth banner
$65.00 (D)

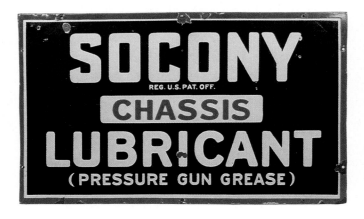

Socony Chassis Lubricant (pressure gun grease)
Standard Oil Company; New York
30" x 18", white, red & blue, porcelain sign
$120.00 (B)

Socony Motor Oil
Standard Oil Company
New York
15" diameter, white, red & blue,
porcelain pump sign
$425.00 (B)

Ask For **Socony Motor Oil**
Standard Oil Company
New York
15" x 15", white, red & blue, porcelain pump sign
$90.00 (B)

The New **Socony Banner Gasoline** The Best Popular Priced Gasoline
Standard Oil Company; New York
99" x 34", white & red, cloth banner
$75.00 (D)

Courtesy of Gene Sonnen

Socony Air-Craft Oils
Standard Oil Company of New York
red, white & blue, porcelain sign
$1,425.00–$1,800.00 (C)

Gold Star Pure Pennsylvania
(Gold Star with derrick art at center)
Star Oil Company
30" diameter, blue, red, white & gold,
porcelain two-sided sign
$375.00 (B)

Sterling Gasoline (British pound sign at center)
A Quaker State Product
Quaker State
11½" x 10", black, yellow, white & red,
porcelain pump sign
$360.00 (B)

We Sell **Sterling Motor** (British pound sign at center)
A Quaker State Product
Quaker State
rectangular black, yellow, white & red, metal sign
$110.00 (B)

Positively No Smoking
Sun Oil Company
20" x 8", white & red, porcelain sign
$100.00–$150.00 (C)

Blue Sunoco (logo arrow art)
Sun Oil Company
Philadelphia, Pennsylvania
Sun Oil merged with Sunray DX in the late 1960s.
19" x 22", red, white, yellow & blue, porcelain sign
$195.00 (B)

Blue Sunoco
Form A 2157 Made in U.. S. A.
Sun Oil Company
Philadelphia, Pennsylvania
12¼" x 8", yellow & blue, porcelain pump sign
$220.00 (B)

Blue Sunoco 190
Sun Oil Company
Philadelphia, Pennsylvania
15" x 12", yellow, blue, white & red,
porcelain pump sign
$175.00–$225.00 (C)

Tenneco
14¾" x 9½", blue, white & red, porcelain sign
$35.00 (B)

Independent Automobile Dealers Ass'n Inc./*member Texas*
9" diameter, red, blue & gold, celluloid plaque
$25.00 (B)

Texaco (logo star in center) Motor Oil
The Texas Company
Port Arthur, Texas
red, white, green & black, porcelain flange sign
$1,100.00–$1,350.00 (C)

Clean, Clear Golden **Texaco Motor Oil**
(logo star at top center)
The Texas Company
Port Arthur, Texas
red, white, green, yellow & black,
tombstone" porcelain flange sign
$1,100.00–$1,350.00 (C)

Texaco (logo star in center)
The Texas Company
Port Arthur, Texas
15" diameter, black, white, green & red,
porcelain sign
(this sign attached to the front of a lube machine)
$175.00 (B)

Texaco (logo star in center)
The Texas Company
Port Arthur, Texas
15" diameter, black, white, green &
red, porcelain pump sign
$225.00 (C)

Sky Chief Marine Texaco Gasoline Super-Charged with Petrox
(logo star at left-center)
The Texas Company
Port Arthur, Texas
(Even though this sign and the Sky Chief Su-preme sign look
very similar, the interest from marine collectors and the fact that
marine signs are scarcer make these two prices very different!)
12" x 18", black, white, green & red, porcelain pump sign
$600.00 (B)

Sky Chief Su-preme Texaco Gasoline Super-Charged with Petrox
(logo star at left-center)
Made in U. S. A./3-10-66
The Texas Company
Port Arthur, Texas
10" x 15", black, white, green & red, porcelain pump sign
$100.00–$125.00 (C)

Sky Chief Texaco Gasoline *(logo star at left-center)*
3-10-47
The Texas Company
Port Arthur, Texas
12" x 18", black, white, green & red, porcelain pump sign
$90.00 (B)

Texaco Agent The Texas Company *(logo star at center-top)*
3-35 at lower right of sign
The Texas Company
Port Arthur, Texas
10⅝" x 12½", black, white, green & red, porcelain sign
$425.00 (B)

Texaco Cyr Oil Company Distributor
(logo star at center-top)
10-6-55 at lower right of sign
circa 1955
The Texas Company
Port Arthur, Texas
11" x 12½", black, white, green & red, porcelain sign
$400.00 (B)

Texaco W. F. Coe Consignee
(logo star at center-top)
10-9-46 at lower right of sign
circa 1946
The Texas Company
Port Arthur, Texas
10½" x 12½", black, white, green & red porcelain sign
$400.00 (B)

Texaco Gasoline Motor Oil
(logo star at center)
The Texas Company
Port Arthur, Texas
42" diameter, black, white, green & red,
porcelain two-sided sign
$450.00 (B)

Texaco Ethyl
(logo star at center-top)
The Texas Company
Port Arthur, Texas
round, black, white, green & red, metal two-sided sign
$600.00–$800.00 (C)

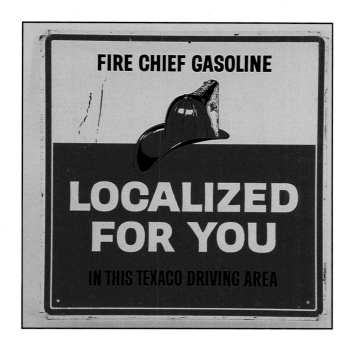

Fire Chief Gasoline (fireman's hat at center top)
Localized for You in this Texaco Driving Area
The Texas Company
Port Arthur, Texas
15½" x 16", black, white & red, painted tin sign
$55.00 (D)

Texaco Marine Lubricants (logo star at left & right)
featuring art of seagulls at top and ships, boats and buoys at bottom
Made in U. S. A. 147
The Texas Company; Port Arthur, Texas
(This sign is very rare and in very good condition, beware of reproductions.)
30" x 15", black, white, green & red, porcelain sign
$1,725.00 (B)

Texaco Inc. Long Beach Airport (NCT-3) SEC-19 S4 12W (logo star at left)
The Texas Company; Port Arthur, Texas
48" x 12", black, white, green & red, porcelain sign
$325.00 (B)

Red plane with **Texaco** *logos on wings and tail fin*
The Texas Company
Port Arthur, Texas
18½" x 15½", framed print
$95.00 (D)

Texaco Fire-Chief Gasoline
with fireman's hat and logo star
3-2-58 in lower left corner
circa 1958; The Texas Company
Port Arthur, Texas
8" x 12", black, white, yellow,
green & red, painted metal sign
$95.00 (D)

Texaco Marine White Gasoline
(logo featured in center of ship's wheel)
circa 1954
The Texas Company; Port Arthur, Texas
12" x 18", black, white, green & red, porcelain sign
$425.00 (B)

Havoline All Temperature Motor Oil/*Change Oil*
Now (Oil Can with Texaco logo featured at left)
circa 1950
The Texas Company
Port Arthur, Texas
17" x 10", black, white, yellow,
green & red, painted tin sign
$85.00 (D)

No Smoking (Texaco logo featured at each end of sign)
Made in U. S. A. 3-40
The Texas Company
Port Arthur, Texas
23" x 4", black, white, green & red, porcelain sign
$110.00 (C)

Drain and Refill With Clean, Clear Golden **Texaco Motor Oil**
art of pouring oil at left
The Texas Company
Port Arthur, Texas
15" diameter, black, white & yellow, porcelain pump sign
$250.00 (B)

Free Crankcase Service Refill With **Texaco Motor Oil**
art of pouring oil and Texaco logo at center bottom
The Texas Company; Port Arthur, Texas
30" x 30", black, white, red, green
& yellow, porcelain sign
$250.00–$375.00 (C)

Get It Now, **Texaco PT Antifreeze**
(featuring art of oil can at left and blustery wind blowing fall leaves)
The Texas Company
Port Arthur, Texas
13¾" x 16½", black, blue, white, red, green & yellow,
die-cut cardboard sign
$95.00 (D)

Courtesy of Gene Sonnen

Authorized **Thoma Glass** Sales & Service
white, yellow & blue, porcelain sign
$1,225.00–$1,475.00 (C)

Quality **Tokheim** Gasoline Pumps
red & white, porcelain pump sign
$375.00–$500.00 (C)

Tide Water Associated Oil Co
/Tydol/Veedol/
Gasoline/Motor oil
blue, white, yellow & green
porcelain sign
$450.00–$750.00 (C)

Time Super Gasoline
featuring clock in center with hands at 1:50
9¼" x 14⅛", black, white & red, porcelain pump sign
$325.00 (B)

Triple Diamond International Service
42" diameter, red, black, blue & white, porcelain sign
$155.00 (D)

Tractor Motor Oil *Reduces Friction Saves Wear*
(Art of farm scene to left and oil derrick at right)
embossed painted metal sign
$150.00–$375.00 (C)

Tydol Gasoline
The Tide Water Oil Company
New York, New York
(This company, founded in 1887, changed its name to Getty in the mid 1960s.)
19½" x 12", black, white & red, die-cut cardboard sign
$100.00 (B)

Tydol Flying A *(art of A with wings at center bottom)*
The Tide Water Oil Company
New York, New York
9¾" diameter, black, white, cream, green & red, metal sign
$170.00 (B)

*Fill up with **Giant Power,** Puts Wings on your Car!*
artwork of a Tydol Gas Station with a Giant holding the flying A
symbol with one hand and pushing a car along with the other
The Tide Water Oil Company; New York, New York
79" x 34", four-color, cloth banner
$195.00 (D)

Tydol *man carrying oil can*
The Tide Water Oil Company
New York, New York
9¾" x 14", cream, yellow & black, two-sided painted metal sign
$175.00 (B)

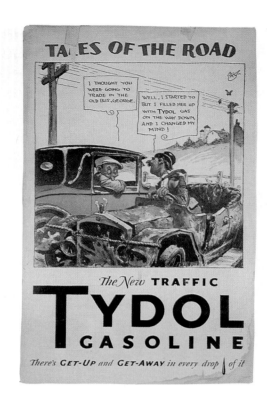

Tales of the Road **Tydol Gasoline** Ads
The Tide Water Oil Company; New York, New York
14" x 22", black, white, & red, set of 4 cardboard signs
$350.00 (B)

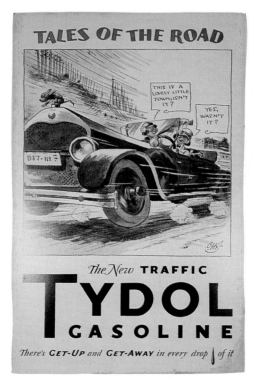

Royal Triton America's Finest Motor Oil!
Art of Oil Can at top
Union 76
black, white, gold & red, metal lollipop two-sided sign
$300.00–$500.00 (C)

Union 76 Certified Car Condition Service
Union Oil Company
22" diameter, black, white, orange & red,
porcelain sign
$145.00 (C)

Royal 76 Gasoline
Union Oil Company
11½" diameter, blue, white & orange,
porcelain pump sign
$80.00 (B)

United Motors Service (art of car in center)
sign was originally neon/tubing missing
United Motors
(Although this sign is an original, these signs are
currently being reproduced with no indication in the
design that they are new.)
36"x 20¾", black, white & orange, porcelain sign
$600.00 (B)

Sherlock Holmes
and Dr. Watson

WINNING COMBINATIONS

YOU and UNITED MOTORS LINES

For our part, here's what we bring to the *winning combination:* products that are used as original equipment on the country's leading cars, trucks and buses; products that are in use on so many *millions* of vehicles today that the parts-and-service potential is almost limitless; products whose preferential position insures a strong and continuing market, month after month, year after year. If you are interested in a *permanent* business, with year-round profits, talk to your United Motors distributor, or write directly to us.

UNITED MOTORS SERVICE
Division of General Motors Corporation
General Motors Building, Detroit 2, Michigan

DELCO Batteries
AC Gauges, Speedometers
   and Rebuilt Fuel Pumps
DELCO Auto Radios
SAGINAW Jacks
MORAINE Engine Bearings
DELCO Radio Parts
HYATT Roller Bearings
DELCO Home Radios
   and Television
INLITE Brake Lining
DUREX Gasoline Filters

HARRISON Heaters
DELCO Shock Absorbers
NEW DEPARTURE
   Ball Bearings
GUIDE Lamps
HARRISON Thermostats
DELCO-REMY Starting,
   Lighting and Ignition
KLAXON Horns
HARRISON Radiators
ROCHESTER Carburetors
DELCO Hydraulic Brakes

UNITED SERVICE MOTORS

An Irving-Cloud Publication
MARCH, 1950

65

Courtesy of Gene Sonnen

Authorized **United Motors Service/**
Delco-Remy/Klaxon
orange, black & white, porcelain sign
$2,250.00–$2,650.00 (C)

Photograph of **U. S. Tire's** *display of quart oil cans*
U. S. Tire Company
(These black and white photographs
are also being newly printed.)
12" x 10", black & white framed photograph
$70.00 (B)

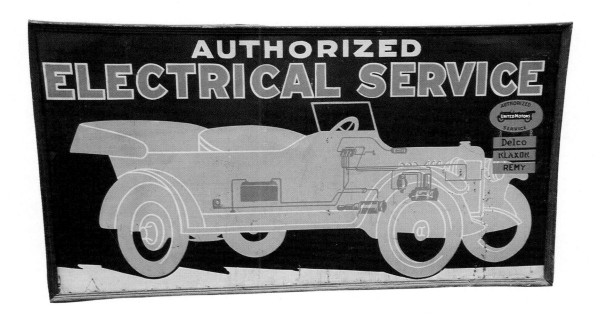

Authorized **Electrical Service**
Authorized United Motors Service
Delco Klaxon Remy
8' wide rectangular orange gold black & white metal self-framed sign
$4,500.00 (C)

U. S. Tires
U. S. Tire Company
14¾" x 11¾", blue, yellow & white frosted glass sign
$35.00 (B)

United States Tires Sales & Service Depot
U. S. Tire Company
20½" x 29¼", blue, orange & white wood
frame & painted metal sign
$250.00 (C)

Courtesy of Gene Sonnen

United Tires
blue & white, tin sign
$75.00–$100.00 (C)

Now in Sealed Quart Tins/**Valvoline Motor Oil**/for your protection
Valvoline Oil Co.
rectangular green, black, silver & white metal sign
$450.00 (D)

General Violet Ray Gasoline
48" diameter violet, red, black & white porcelain sign
$900.00–$1,450.00 (C)

VW *(logo in center) Service*
Volkswagen
25 x 30", blue & white porcelain sign
$235.00 (B)

Courtesy of Gene Sonnen

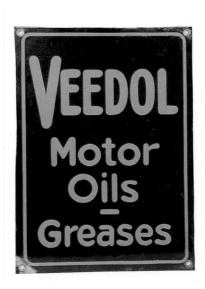

Veedol Motor Oils/Greases
Tide Water
New York, New York
10" x 14", orange & black porcelain sign
$250.00 (B)

Veedol Motor Oil *(with logo of V with wings)*
Tide Water
New York, New York
black, red & white, tin flanged sign
$450.00–$550.00 (C)

THE SATURDAY EVENING POST

October 16, 1943

First Class Fighting Man

He's won a place beside the Marines who made that deathless stand at Wake Island . . .

. . . he's comrade to MacArthur's gallant handful on Bataan, who repeatedly stopped a ten-against-one Jap juggernaut in its tracks — *and then attacked* . . .

. . . he's made of the same stuff as Chennault's Flying Tigers in Burma, who laughed at the odds against them, and wrote history with the smoky trails of shot-down foes . . .

And it's a cinch those glory-covered scrappers are grinning in admiration as the lad on the tanker takes on Nazi dive-bombers and sub-

marines as matter-of-factly as he takes a trick at the wheel.

Courage? He's got it to spare. Our fighting forces, our whole war effort, depend largely on OIL — and come hell or high water, typhoons or torpedoes, the tankerman will see that the oil gets through.

This fleet of hard-driven tankers and their loyal crews was built up by America's petroleum industry. But shortly after Pearl Harbor, the fleet was turned over to Uncle Sam — together with its commanders and their men. It was a ready-made task force in the Battle for Oil

— the battle on which the outcome of *many* battles would depend.

The ships of Tide Water Associated united with the ships of the other oil companies to join the colors. And our hands united, too, in many vital war tasks. Fighting as one, we have, where necessary, pooled our facilities, our equipment, our processes and our patents.

The fight will be hard — it may be long. But the United States has a united people. Standing together, we cannot fall.

TIDE WATER ASSOCIATED OIL COMPANY
New York • Tulsa • San Francisco

WORLD'S LARGEST REFINERS OF PENNSYLVANIA OILS

TIDE WATER ASSOCIATED

OIL IS AMMUNITION - USE IT WISELY

★ BUY WAR BONDS AND STAMPS!

White Trucks Parts-Service
36" x 28¼", blue, orange and white, porcelain sign
$600.00 (B)

Courtesy of Gene Sonnen

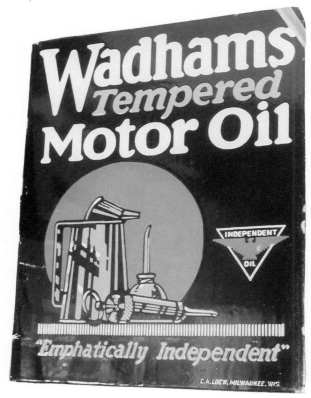

Courtesy of Gene Sonnen

Wadhams Tempered Motor Oil
*black, orange, yellow & white, porcelain
flanged sign*
$1,850.00–$2,000.00 (C)

Gasoline White Eagle and Keynoil
30" wide, black, red & white, porcelain sign
$625.00–$800.00 (C)

Wadhams Tempered Motor Oil
*Art of oil glass container at right and metal oil cans at left
Wadhams Oil Company; Milwaukee, Wisconsin
84" x 18", white, yellow, red & black, wood framed painted tin sign*
$135.00 (D)

White Rose
White Rose Company
17½" x 18", yellow, black and
white, porcelain sign
$150.00 (C)

Courtesy of Gene Sonnen

White Star Staroleum Gasoline
White Star Company
30" diameter, blue and white,
porcelain two-sided sign
$450.00 (B)

Wil-Flo Motor Oil at 30° below
(featuring art of snow scene and early auto)
Mid-West Oil Company
dark & light blue, red & white, tin sign
$1050.00–$1,300.00 (C)

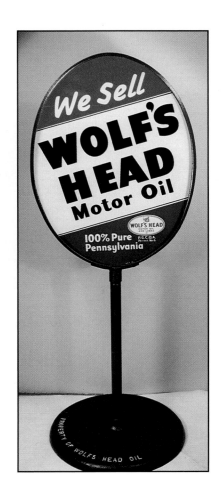

We Sell **Wolf's Head Motor Oil**
59" tall, red, black & white lollipop two-sided curb sign
cast base with raised lettering
circa 1953
(restored) $400.00 (C)

Zero Flo *Pours at 35° below/paraffin base motor oil/40 cents per quart*
28" x 20" black, yellow & white embossed painted tin sign
$155.00 (C)

Wonder Worker *Motor Car Necessities (art of driver on each side)*
no company
36" x 10", red, black, green & white painted tin sign
$225.00 (D)

The way people choose to display their collections never ceases to amaze me. Some people have fences on which to hang their signs. Others have sign houses, with signs covering both the inside and outside, while some have old barns full of the stuff.

John and Vicki Mahan of Murray, Kentucky, have a house full of some really neat signs. But they also found an old log cabin about to be torn down and decided they had the ideal spot for it in their back yard. And of course what's an old building without old signs and advertising pieces. John and Vicki not only recycle great old signs but also the building housing many of them. They had the cabin torn down log by log and re-assembled at their home. Way to go John & Vicki. It all fits together and looks great!

Courtesy of John & Vicki Mahan

Mobilgas Pegasus
Socony-Vacuum
shield shaped blue, red & white painted tin sign
*(this huge sign hangs on the exterior of the re-
assembled log cabin at John & Vicki Mahan's home)*
$350.00 (C)

EN-AR-CO/*White Rose Open sign*
Small boy holding board announcing business hours
cast base
*(Even though this sign is in rough condition, its
uniqueness makes an interesting conversation piece
on the front porch of the log cabin.)*
$275.00 (C)

*Above the Mobilgas sign in the
peak of the cabin these signs are
displayed:*

Standard *(torch in center)*
Oval red, blue & white metal sign
$275.00 (C)

Standard Services
blue dropped out letters
$200.00 (C)

CONTAINERS

Today's avid collector of petroleum containers may have thousands of cans, bottles, and more in their collection. Many new to the hobby will want to know where all these containers have been and who in the world would save an empty oil can for thirty years or more? Well the question has multiple answers. Some rare individuals with the foresight to recognize a valuable piece of Americana have saved these treasures. Many a rare can has been given a second life as an organizing container for nails, screws, nuts and bolts in a handyman's garage until they are sold at a yard sale to a lucky petroleum collectibles hunter. Another surprising source has been the can companies themselves and their retired employees. By saving examples of their craft, these folks have helped to complete many a collection of mint condition containers.

Recently collectors have branched off from the mainline containers such as quart oil cans and bottles into the by-products of the petroleum industry. Bug spray containers and applicators, farm aids, roofing products, "Gulfwax" boxes and more are becoming sought after collectibles. The varieties and the availability of these products seems endless.

Today, collectors that are thinking into the future of this field are beginning to pick up on plastic containers now readily available. These containers are coming under the scrutiny of ecologists and environmentalists as an enemy to our ecosystem and as such may be doomed to extinction.

Some of the earliest of oil containers were barrels. They were identified by paper labels affixed to the ends. There are collectors that specialize in these early paper collectibles and the dies that were used to print them.

When the end-user at the gas station became the marketing target, oil began to require a more user-friendly size container. Another method of marketing was needed. Beside the curb dispensers or oil carts (see page 80 in the pump chapter), early oil began to be distributed mainly in the five gallon steel containers and quart glass containers. Many of the early quart glass containers were embossed with the oil company logo (see page 268). This allowed the buyer to visually inspect the product and the embossing eliminated the problem of an oil damaged label. However, the durability of these containers led to their demise. The ability to refill left the good name established by the oil company at risk. Although the glass containers were breakable, they did not deteriorate with age or exposure. This allowed them to be reused over and over. In fact many glass oil bottles are still turning up today brought up from the basements of old bulk dealers. An unethical jobber could refill his Shell-Penn bottles, for example, with an oil of lesser quality and continue to market the product as Shell. This pirating practice of selling lesser quality oil as premium brought about the end of a refillable, resealable container. There was still a smaller field of refillables left operating, but mostly for lower grades and lesser known brands of oil.

The oil industry's answer to the pirating of their logos came in the form of factory sealed cans. Some early sealed tins make note of the fact: "our containers are sealed at the factory assuring a quality product." These early oil cans were available mainly in the one quart and five quart sizes. Five quart cans were eventually phased out and the market was dominated by the one quart can. Five quart cans are generally more valuable than the more common quart size can. But this is not always the case. There are some five quart cans that are quite common. You must also take into account company name, lettering, logos, artwork used and the number of colors employed to decorate the cans, and of course, condition.

Flying A Americo Motor Oil *can*
American Oil Company
1 gallon tin
$30.00 (B)

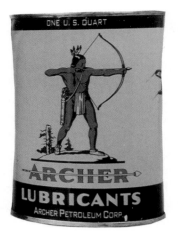

Archer Lubricants *can*
(featuring Indian figure art)
Archer Petroleum Company
1 quart, 4" diameter x 5½" tall
circa 1935–1945
$35.00 (B)

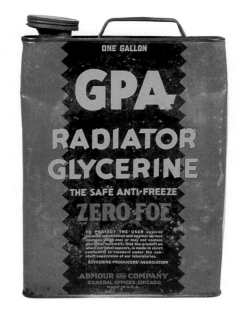

GPA Radiator Glycerine Zero-Foe *can*
Armour and Company
Chicago, Illinois
1 gallon tin, 11½" tall
$25.00–$75.00 (B*)

Standard Hand Separator Oil *can*
(featuring illustration of an oil separator)
The Atlantic Refining Company
Philadelphia, Pennsylvania
half gallon tin, 2¼" deep x 9" tall
$20.00 (B)

Atlantic Motor Grease *can*
(featuring crossed arrow Atlantic logo)
The Atlantic Refining Company
Philadelphia, Pennsylvania
5 lb. tin, 6½" diameter x 5¼" tall
$25.00 (D)

Atlantic Motor Grease can (featuring crossed arrow Atlantic logo)
The crossed arrow logo was used from 1915 to the mid thirties
The Atlantic Refining Company
Philadelphia, Pennsylvania
1 gallon tin, 11½"
$50.00 (B)

Polarine transmission lubricant can
The Atlantic Refining Company
Philadelphia, Pennsylvania
5 lb. tin, 5" x 8"
$65.00 (B)

Capitol Motor Oil Paraffin Base can with
US Capitol building art behind lettering
The Atlantic Refining Company
Philadelphia, Pennsylvania
(featuring crossed arrow Atlantic logo)
2 gallon tin, 7" x 10"
$20.00 (D)

Atlantic Motor Oil can
(featuring a red airplane on a blue chevron)
The Atlantic Refining Company
Philadelphia, Pennsylvania
1 quart tin, 4" diameter x 5½" tall
$25.00 (B)

Farmer Allerton's Axle Grease tin
(featuring artwork of a farmer with a bucket and rake)
Allerton Lubricant Company
Chicago, Illinois
4¼" diameter
$35.00 (B)

Be Square Auto Oil tin
(featuring B in square logo)
Barnsdall Refining Company
New York, New York
(Barnsdall Refining Company was
purchased by DX in 1952)
half gallon tin, 8" x 5¾"
$70.00 (B)

Barnsdall lubricant, America's first refiner tin
(featuring B in square logo)
Barnsdall Refining Company
New York, New York
5 lb tin, 8" x 5¾"
$20.00 (B)

Barnsdall motor oil, America's first refiner tin
(featuring B in square logo)
Barnsdall Refining Company
New York, New York
5 lb tin, 6⅜" diameter" x 9½" tall
$80.00 (B)

Barnsdall stabilized motor oil, America's first
refiner tin (featuring B in square logo)
Barnsdall Refining Company
New York, New York
(Barnsdall Refining Company began
operations in the 1920's and then in the
1940's started using the Bareco
(Barnsdall Refining CO.) name. They shut
down operations in the early 1950s.)
4" diameter x 5½" tall
$60.00 (B)

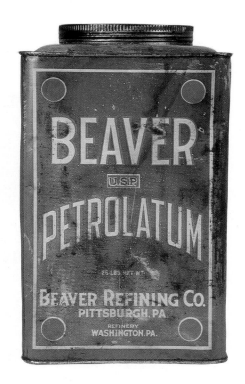

Bellube tin
(featuring logo of a bell with an oil derrick in the center)
The Bell Oil and Gas Company
Grandfield and Tulsa, Oklahoma
10 lb. tin, 7½" diameter x 8" tall
$35.00 (D)

Beaver Petrolatum tin
Beaver Refining Company
Pittsburgh, Pennsylvania
25 lb. tin, 13" tall
$45.00 (B)

Use **Champlin Oils**, Motor Oil tin
(featuring Champlin logo)
Champlin Refining Company
Enid, Oklahoma
circa 1928–1946
5 quart tin, 7" diameter x 9½" tall
$25.00 (D)

Brunswick Motor Oil tin
100% pure Pennsylvania Oil
Brunswick Oil Company
Philadelphia, Pennsylvania
2 gallon tin, 9½" x 8½"
$50.00 (B)

Use **Champlin Oils**, Motor Oil tin
(featuring Champlin logo)
Champlin Refining Company
Enid, Oklahoma
1 quart tin
$50.00 (B)

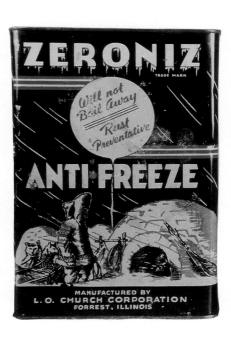

Zeroniz Anti-freeze tin
(featuring Eskimo & Igloo artwork)
L. O. Church Corporation
Forrest, Illinois
1 gallon tin, 6½" x 5½"
$40.00 (B)

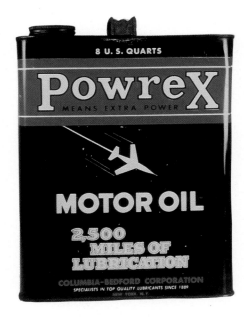

Power X Motor Oil tin, 2,500 miles of lubrication
(featuring jet plane art)
Specialists in Top Quality Lubricants since 1889
Columbia-Bedford Corporation
New York, New York
8 quart tin, 11" tall
$25.00 (D)

Cities Service Oils Servoil Auto tin
(featuring logo in the center)
Cities Service Oil Company
Tulsa, Oklahoma
1 gallon tin, 7½" x 10¼"
(This Cities Service logo dates from 1957–1960. Cities
Service began as a public utility in the early part of this
century, but became Citco in the mid 1960s.)
$35.00 (C)

Conoco Oil tin (featuring triangle logo)
Continental Oil Company
Denver, Colorado
(Conoco began using this logo in 1929 and continued until 1950 when the triangle outline was dropped. Conoco was once owned by Standard Oil and then purchased by Dupont Chemicals in the 1980s.)
1 gallon tin, 8" x 10¼"
$75.00 (B)

Conoco Transmission Grease tin (featuring minuteman)
Continental Oil Company
Denver, Colorado
The Continental Oil Company used this
minuteman from 1913 to 1929.
5 lb. tin, 5½" x 8"
$300.00 (C)

Cushing Grease tin
(featuring Art Deco style logo)
Cushing Refining and Gasoline Co.
Cushing, Oklahoma
5 lb. tin, 5½" diameter x 7½" tall
$40.00 (B)

Cornell Tube Repair Kit tin
Cornell Tire and Rubber Co.
circa 1933
3½" diameter x 8½" tall tin
$95.00 (B)

Deep Rock Air Race tin (featuring airplane artwork)
Deep Rock Oil Corporation
Chicago, Illinois
(Deep Rock Oil was originally established in 1913 in Oklahoma
and then eventually was bought out by Kerr-McGee in the 1950s.)
5 quart tin, 6½" x 9½"
$55.00 (D)

Air Race Motor Oil, Deep Rock tin
(featuring airplane artwork)
Deep Rock Oil Corporation
Chicago, Illinois
circa 1935–1945
1 quart tin, 4" diameter x 5½" tall
$110.00 (B)

Courtesy of Gene Sonnen

Deep Rock Prize Motor Oil tin
Deep Rock Oil Corporation
Chicago, Illinois
1 quart tin, 4" diameter x 5½" tall
$45.00 (D)

Deep Rock tin
Shaffer Oil Refining Company
Chicago, Illinois
half gallon tin
$150.00–$200.00 (C)

Fisk Motor *tune up tin*
Fisk Oil Corporation
16 oz tin, 3¾" x 5⅞"
$45.00 (D)

Genuine **Ford** *Anti-Freeze tin*
(featuring Ford logo lettering)
Ford Motor Company
Dearborn, Michigan
1 gallon tin, 8" x 10"
$130.00 (B)

Franco Motor Oil *tin*
(featuring oil derrick artwork)
Franklin Railway Oil Corporation
Distributed by Dean Phipps Auto Stores
1 gallon tin; $30.00 (B)

Freedom Motor Cycle Oil *tin*
(featuring FOWCO trade mark in center)
The Freedom Oil Works Company
Freedom, Pennsylvania
1 gallon tin
$85.00 (D)

Tiger Oil *tin (featuring tiger head art in the center)*
Gamble Auto Supply Company
100% Pennsylvania Oil
5 gallon easy pour tin, 14¼" diameter x 16¾" tall
$225.00 (D)

Gebharts Gold Comet Motor Oil *tin*
(featuring comet art)
100% Pennsylvania Oil
1 quart tin, 4" diameter x 5½" tall
$75.00 (B)

Bengol *tin, Pure Pennsylvania Heat Resisting Lubricants tin*
(featuring Bengal tiger head art)
The Gibson Company
Indianapolis, Indiana
100% Pennsylvania Oil
5 gallon easy pour tin, 14¼" diameter x 16¾" tall
$275.00 (B)

Golden Leaf Motor Oil *tin*
(featuring gold oak leaf art)
100% Pennsylvania Oil
Golden State Oil Company of California
1 quart tin, 4" diameter x 5½" tall
$30.00 (B)

Grand Champion Special Motor Oil *tin*
(featuring race cars & drivers art)
2 gallon tin, 10¼" tall
$145.00 (B)

Gree-soff Pure Linseed Oil compound
Automobile Soap tin
(featuring automobile art in center)
circa 1930
6¼" x 5¼"; $65.00 (D)

Supreme Auto Oil tin
Gulf Refining Company
Boston/New York/Philadelphia/Houston/Atlanta/New Orleans/
Louisville
(Gulf Oil Company, Pittsburgh, Pennsylvania, was founded in
1901 and opened their first official gas station, built to sell
gasolene, in 1913. They were purchased by Chevron in 1984
who sold operations in many states to BP.)
1 gallon tin, 8½" x 5½" tall
$65.00 (C)

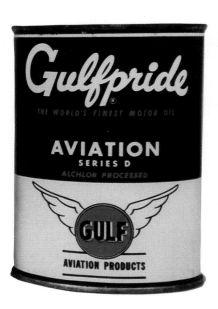

Gulf Supreme Motor Oil tin (featuring Gulf logo)
Gulf Refining Company
Boston/New York/Philadelphia/Houston/Atlanta/
New Orleans/Louisville
1 quart refinery sealed, tamper proof tin,
4" diameter x 5½" tall
$30.00 (C)

Gulfpride Aviation Series D Motor Oil tin
(featuring Gulf logo with wings)
Gulf Refining Company
Boston/New
York/Philadelphia/Houston/Atlanta/
New Orleans/Louisville
1 quart tin, 4" diameter x 5½" tall
$90.00 (B)

Supreme Gulf Motor Oil "W" tin
(featuring Gulf logo)
Gulf Refining Company
Boston/New York/Philadelphia/Houston/
Atlanta/New/Orleans/Louisville
1 gallon tin, 8" x 10"
$40.00 (B)

Gulf Cold Flo Antifreeze tin
(featuring Gulf logo and cars in snow art)
Gulf Refining Company
Boston/New York/Philadelphia/
Houston/Atlanta/New Orleans/Louisville
1 quart tin, 4" diameter x 5½" tall
$75.00 (B)

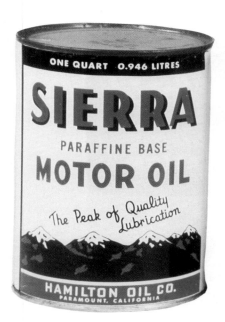

Sierra Paraffin Base Motor Oil tin
(featuring mountains artwork)
Hamilton Oil Company
Paramount, California
1 quart tin, 4" diameter x 5½" tall
$100.00 (B)

Hancock Old Black Joe Grease tin
(featuring black face artwork)
John Hancock Oil Company
Twin Cities
1 lb tin, 4" tall
$110.00 (B)

Whiz *Silicone Formula Lusterize Long Lasting Wax Veneer tin
(featuring car and spray can art)
R. M. Hollingshead Corporation
(Mr. Hollingshead owned a service station and some land
during the depression year of 1933 when money was
scarce. He was granted a patent for a new form of
entertainment he called the "drive-in theater.")
Camden, New Jersey
1 gallon tin, 6½" x 9½"
$30.00 (D)*

Harris Premium Outboard Motor Oil *tin
(featuring Harris Oils logo)
A. W. Harris Oil Company
Providence, Rhode Island
1 quart cone top tin, 4" diameter x 9" tall
$95.00 (B)*

Whiz *Separator Oil tin
R. M. Hollingshead Corporation
Camden, New Jersey
1 quart tin, 8¾" tall
$65.00 (D)*

Motor Oil, *Dependable Lubrication For Your
Motor tin (featuring #8 race car art)
Home Oil Company (HOCO)
Ripley, Tennessee
half gallon tin, 8" x 5½"
$120.00 (B)*

Scholl's Axle Grease
(horse drawn cart with black people in center of can) has the
longest mileage record of any grease made
Independent Oil Company
Mansfield, Ohio
5¾" diameter x 6½" tall
$30.00 (B)

Havoline Oil tin
Indian Refining Company
New York, New York
(The early Indian Company was purchased by Texaco in 1931.
The Indian Logo was used until the early 1940s
when Texaco sold Indian as their 3rd grade, low price gas.
It is interesting to note that Texaco still sells Havoline Oil.)
1 gallon tin, 6" x 10½"
$75.00 (D)

P-H Lubricant tin
(scenery of Bucktail Trail in Pennsylvania in the center of the can)
Industrial Oil Corporation
Warren, Pennsylvania
5 lb tin, 6" diameter x 7½" tall
$25.00 (B)

Pennsylvania 100% pure Motor Oil tin (scenery of Bucktail Trail in
Pennsylvania in the center of the can) Penn Hills Brand
Industrial Oil Corporation
Warren, Pennsylvania
1 quart tin, 4" diameter x 5½" tall
$130.00 (B)

Joco Oils Motor Oil tin
Joplin Oil Company
Joplin, Missouri
half gallon tin
$65.00 (B)

Johnson Motor Oil tin
Johnson Oil Refining Company
Chicago, Illinois
5 quart tin
$110.00–$165.00 (C)

Giant Oil tin (featuring black oil blot art)
Kalite Oil Company
Tulsa, Oklahoma
1 gallon tin, 8" x 10"
$35.00 (B)

Katz Motor Oil tin
(art of cat driving automobile)
Katz Drug Company
Kansas City, Missouri
5 gallon tin
$95.00 (C)

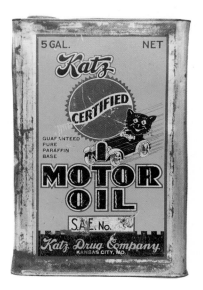

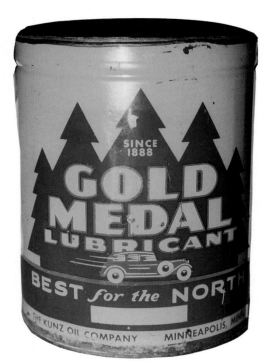

Gold Medal Lubricant/Since 1888
The Kunz Oil Company
Minneapolis, Minnesota
grease pail tin
$95.00–$115.00 (C)

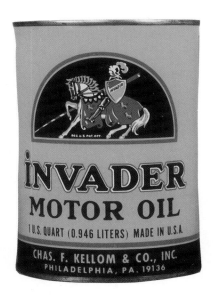

Invader Motor Oil tin (featuring knight on horseback art)
Chas. F. Kellom & Co., Inc.
Philadelphia, Pennsylvania 19136
circa 1950s
1 quart tin, 4" diameter x 5½" tall
$40.00 (C)

Magnolene Motor Heavy tin (featuring
magnolia logo art)
Magnolia Petroleum Company
Beaumont, Texas
1 gallon tin, 6" x 10¾"
$65.00 (B)

Trop-Artic Motor Oil tin
(one side features auto in the arctic & the
other side shows auto in the tropics)
circa 1915–1925
Manhattan Oil Company
St. Paul, Minnesota
(This company was purchased by Phillips in 1934.)
half gallon tin, 6¼" tall
$1,355.00 (B)

Trop-Artic Motor Oil tin (Satisfies from Pole to Pole)
(one side features auto in the arctic & the other side
shows auto in the tropics)
circa 1915–1925
Manhattan Oil Company
St. Paul, Minnesota
1 quart cone top with screw lid tin, 9" tall
$110.00 (B)

Marathon Grease tin (featuring Marathon Products runner logo. Marathon used this logo from 1915 through the 1930s.)
Marathon Oil Company
Tulsa, Oklahoma
10 lb tin, 7¼" diameter x 9" tall
$50.00 (B)

French Auto Oil tin, Always Good, try It
(featuring race car and driver on track artwork)
Marshall Oil Company
5 gallon tin, 9⅜" x 14"
$440.00 (B)

Ace High Motor Oil tin
(featuring race car & airplane artwork)
circa 1935–1945
Midwest Oil Company
Minneapolis, Minnesota
1 quart tin, 4" diameter x 6¾" tall
$75.00 (D)

Red Indian Motor Oil tin (featuring Indian chief artwork)
McCall Frontenac Oil Company Limited
(Red Indian globes are being illegally reproduced now.
Make sure what your are buying is authentic.)
1 quart tin, 4" diameter x 6¾" tall
$65.00 (B)

Penn-Aero Triple Filtered Motor Oil *tin, 35¢ per quart*
(featuring propeller artwork)
100% Pure Pennsylvania Oil
Mid-West Oil Company
Kansas City, Kansas
1 quart tin
$135.00 (B)

Viking Chief Motor Oil *tin*
(featuring artwork of a Viking in the
"I" of the word Chief)
Miller Oil Company, Limited
Brantford, Ontario
1 quart tin, 4" diameter x 6¾" tall
$100.00 (B)

MonaMotor Oil *tin*
(featuring a landscape scene with cars & plane)
Monarch Mfg. Company
Council Bluffs, Iowa/San Francisco,
California/Toledo, Ohio
(MonaMotor brand merged with Barnsdall
in the late 1920s.)
half gallon tin
$100.00 (B)

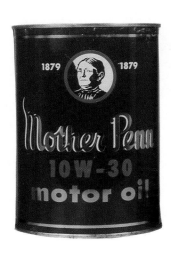

Mother-Penn10W-30 Motor Oil *tin*
(featuring picture of Mother-Penn at top)
1 quart tin, 4" diameter x 5" tall
$65.00 (B)

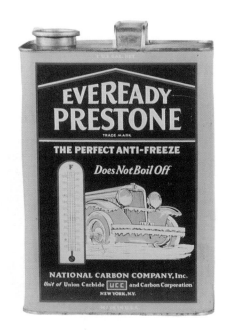

Eveready Prestone The Perfect Antifreeze tin
(featuring a thermometer and car artwork)
National Carbon Company, Inc.
unit of Union Carbide & Carbon Corporation
New York, New York
1 gallon tin with handle and spout on top, 6½" x 9½"
$65.00 (C)

Eveready Prestone The Perfect Antifreeze tin
(featuring a thermometer and car artwork)
National Carbon Company, Inc.
unit of Union Carbide & Carbon Corporation
New York, New York
1 gallon tin, no handle or spout on top,
6½" x 9½"
$45.00 (C)

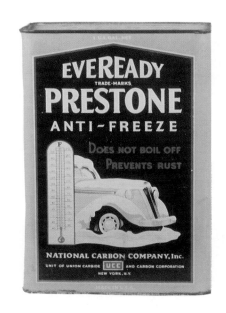

EN-AR-CO Motor Oil tin (featuring company logo at bottom, writing on boy's slate is not in script) See photo on page 151.
The National Refining Company
Cleveland, Ohio
circa 1935–1945
1 quart tin, 4" x 5½"
$35.00 (C)

EN-AR-CO Motor Oil tin
(featuring company logo at top)
The National Refining Company
Cleveland, Ohio
5 gallon easy-pour tin, 14½" diameter x 16¾" tall
$125.00 (C)

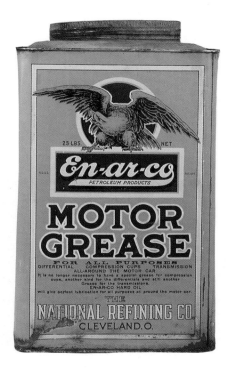

EN-AR-CO Motor Grease tin (featuring eagle art at top)
The National Refining Company
Cleveland, Ohio
25 lb. tin, 8" x 12"
$50.00 (D)

EN-AR-CO Motor Oil tin
(boy with slate featuring script writing was used from 1918–1925)
The National Refining Company
Cleveland, Ohio
1 gallon tin, 8½" x 5½"
$65.00 (D)

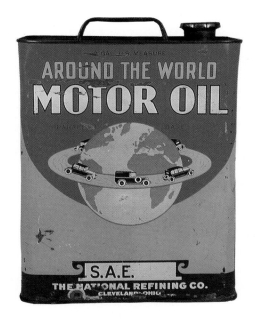

Around the World Motor Oil tin
(featuring globe art)
The National Refining Company
Cleveland, Ohio; circa 1925–1945
2 gallon tin, 8" x 11"
$25.00 (D)

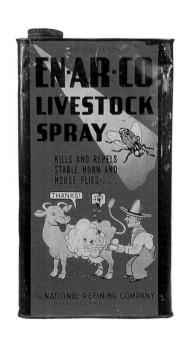

EN-AR-CO Livestock Spray tin
(art of farmer and cow on front)
The National Refining Company
Cleveland, Ohio
1 gallon tin, 6" x 11"
$30.00 (B)

Monogram Oils and Greases tin
The New York Lubrication Oil Company/consolidated
with Columbia Lubricants Company
New York, New York
1 gallon tin, 10" tall
$30.00 (B)

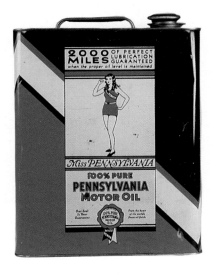

100% Pure Pennsylvania Motor Oil tin
(featuring "Miss Pennsylvania Motor Oil")
no company name
2 gallon tin, 8½" x 10"
$50.00 (B)

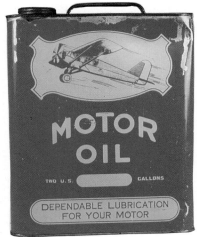

Motor Oil, *dependable lubrication for your motor* tin
(featuring air plane art)
no company name
circa 1925–1945
2 gallon tin, 10½"
$45.00 (D)

The Norse Brands tin
(featuring Viking art)
Norse Company
Kansas City, Missouri
1 gallon tin, 7" x 10½"
$90.00 (B)

Oilzum Motor Oil tin *(featuring man's face in cap and goggles)*
5 quart tin, 6½" diameter x 9½" tall
$130.00 (B)

Captain Parlube Motor Oil *tin*
(featuring mountain scene with car)
Parlube Oil Company
Beckett Bros,
Holmes, Pennsylvania; circa 1925–1945
2 gallon tin, 8½" x 11½"
$125.00 (B)

Auto Sweeping Compound *tin*
(featuring car art ligthograph in center)
Paxson Manufacturing Company
Philadelphia, Pennsylvania
3 quart tin, 5½" x 8¾"
$25.00 (B)

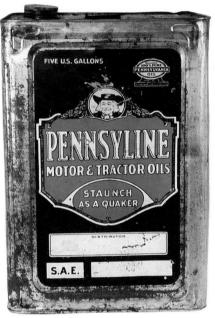

Pennsyline Motor and Tractor Oils *tin*
(featuring Quaker man)
Staunch as a Quaker 100% pure Pennsylvania Oil
5 gallon tin, 9⅜" x 14"
$20.00 (D)

Hi-Temp Dewaxed Triple Filtered Motor Oil *tin*
(featuring thermometer art)
Penn-Central Oil Company, Inc.
Kansas City, Kansas
1 quart tin, 4" x 5½"
$25.00 (C)

Penn-Champ 100% Pure Pennsylvania Motor Oil *tin*
(featuring horse and rider art)
2 gallon tin, 8½" x 10½"
$25.00 (C)

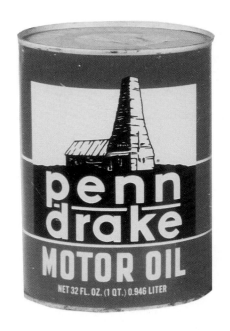

Penn-Drake Motor Oil *tin*
(featuring picture of Drake oil well)
Pennsylvania Refining Company
Butler, Pennsylvania
(Penn-Drake was purchased by Pennzoil in the early 1970s.)
1 quart tin, 4" diameter x 5½" tall
$60.00 (B)

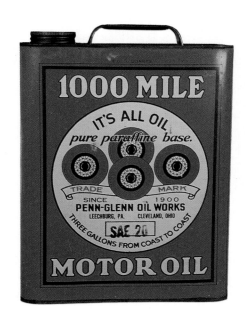

Pennsylvania 100% Motor Oil *tin*
(featuring Pennsylvania scenery along the Bucktail Trail)
Penn Hills Brand
Industrial Oil Corporation
Warren, Pennsylvania; circa 1925–1945
2 gallon tin, 8½" x 11½"
$95.00 (C)

1000 Mile Motor Oil *tin*
(featuring Penn-Glenn trademark)
Penn-Glenn Oil Works
Leechburg, Pennsylvania/Cleveland, Ohio
3 gallon tin, 10½" tall
$20.00 (B)

Pennsylvania Petroleum Products Co.
Philadelphia, Pennsylvania
Defender Motor Oil tin (featuring soldier with rifle)
2 gallon tin, 11½" tall
$100.00 (B)

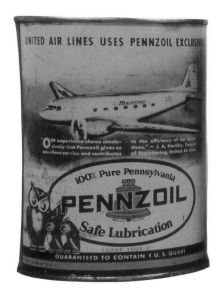

*United Airlines uses **Pennzoil** exclusively tin*
(featuring airplane art at top & 3 owl art at bottom left)
Pennzoil Company
Houston, Texas, Oil City, Pennsylvania
(Pennzoil Gas was renamed Pennzip in 1936 and contin-
ued until the late 1950's. They marketed and transported
gasoline in the 1940s & 1950s.)
1 quart tin, 4" diameter x 5½" tall
$65.00 (B)

Prize Penn *(art of red Thunderbird at top)*
Pennsylvania Super Fine Motor Oil Tin
1 quart tin, 4" diameter x 5½" tall
$25.00 (B)

Pep Boys' Pure as Gold Cup Grease
Pep Boys (Manny, Moe, and Jack)
Philadelphia, Pennsylvania
1 lb tin, 4¼" diameter
$185.00 (B)

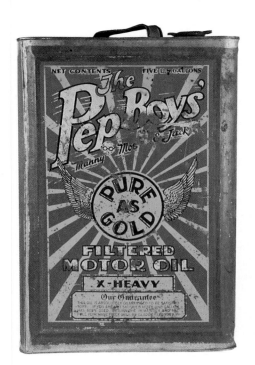

Pep Boys' Pure as Gold Filtered Motor, X-Heavy *tin*
Pep Boys (Manny, Moe, and Jack)
Philadelphia, Pennsylvania
5 gallon tin, 9" x 14"
$90.00 (B)

Quaker Brand Anti-freeze Alcohol *tin*
(with Quaker woman art in center)
Pennsylvania Sugar Co.
Philadelphia, Pennsylvania
2 gallon tin, 9½" x 8½"
$55.00 (C)

Phillips Grease *tin*
(Phillips used the round logo until 1934, however the shield logo did begin appearing around 1930.)
Phillips Petroleum Company
Bartlesville, Oklahoma
(This company was founded in 1917 by Frank Phillips and others. The first station was opened in 1927 in Wichita, Kansas. They had stations in all 50 states at one point in time.)
5 lb. tin, 5¾" diameter x 7½" tall
$20.00 (B)

Pierce Oil Corporation Pennant Oils *tin*
Pierce Oil Corporation
New York, New York
circa 1915–1925
half gallon tin, 6¼" tall
$75.00 (B)

Pennant Oil 4-D Oil *tin*
(the wonder lubricant for Fords)
circa 1915–1925
Pierce Petroleum Corporation
St. Louis, Missouri
(Pierce Petroleum Co. out of St. Louis dates from
approximately 1912–1930, at which time it was
purchased by Sinclair Oil.)
half gallon tin, 8" x 5½"
$45.00 (B)

Thermo *Completely Denatured*
Alcohol Anti-freeze, formula No. 5-188
circa 1915–1925
Publicker Commercial Alcohol Company
Philadelphia, Pennsylvania
1 gallon tin, 9¾" tall
$45.00 (B)

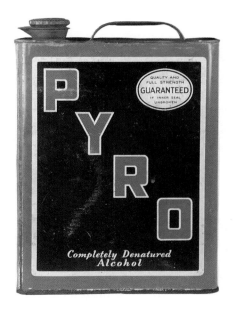

Pyro Completely Denatured Alcohol
1 gallon tin, 8" x 10¼"
$40.00 (C)

Quaker State Heavy Oil tin
Quaker State Oil Refining Co.
Oil City, Pennsylvania, U. S. A.
1 gallon tin, 7½" x 10½"
$65.00 (B)

Duplex Marine Engine Oil tin
(featuring red boat with driver
and buoy in water art)
Quaker State Oil Refining Corp.
Oil City, Pennsylvania
1 quart tin
$90.00 (B)

Quaker State Oil-Well tin, the magic household oil of 1000 uses
Quaker State Oil Refining Corp.
Oil City, Pennsylvania
oiler, 3½" tall
$100.00 (D)

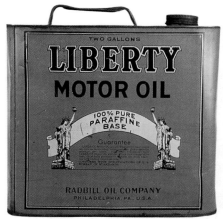

Liberty Motor Oil tin
(pair of Statues of Liberty with banner)
100% pure paraffin base
Radbill Oil Company; Philadelphia, Pennsylvania
2 gallon tin
$95.00 (D)

Thrift-Lube Motor Oil tin (mountain scene and race car art)
100% pure paraffin base motor oil
Radbill Oil Company
Philadelphia, Pennsylvania
2 gallon tin, 9½" x 8½"
$85.00 (C)

Rajah Motor Oil *(with Rajah face at top)*
A Penn-O-Tex Product
5 quart tin
$125.00–$275.00 (C)

Red Hat Motor Oil *tin*
(red hat trademark and logo in center)
*(Red Hat brand was discontinued when Standard Oil
sued claiming copyright infringement of their Red
Crown. Until that suit the Red Hat logo was used by
a group of independent oil men.)*
1 quart tin, 4" diameter x 5" tall
$85.00 (B)

Red Indian Aviation Motor Oil *tin*
(Indian art at top)
1 quart tin, 4" diameter x 6½" tall
$190.00 (B)

Pen-O-Lene Motor Oil *tin*
*100% Pure Pennsylvania Oil logo
Red Trail Oil Company
Mandan, North Dakota
half gallon tin, 8" x 6½"
$40.00 (B)*

Rocket Superfine-Certified Motor Oil tin
(picture of rocket on white background)
1 quart tin, 4" x 5½"
$40.00 (B)

Route 66 Premium Motor Oil
(logo in center)
2 gallon tin, 8½" x 11½"
$25.00 (D)

Shell Motor Oil *(shell clam in center)*
Roxana Petroleum Corporation
St. Louis, Missouri
(Shell Oil purchased Roxana petroleum in 1917,
Shell continued using the Roxana name into the 1920s.)
1 gallon tin, 8" x 11"
$155.00 (D)

Samson Anti-Freeze,
a perfect alcohol-glycerine mixture for automobile cooling systems
Samson Products Company; Philadelphia, Pennsylvania
1 gallon tin, 9¾" tall
circa 1915–1925
$75.00 (D)

Golden Shell Motor Oil *(shell clam logo in center)*
Shell Oil Company
Houston, Texas
A Division of "Royal Dutch Shell"
5 quart tin, 6½" diameter x 9½" tall
$45.00 (B)

Shell Motor Oil
(shell clam logo bottom left)
Shell Oil Company
Houston, Texas
A Division of "Royal Dutch Shell"
1 gallon tin, 9" x 7"
$45.00 (D)

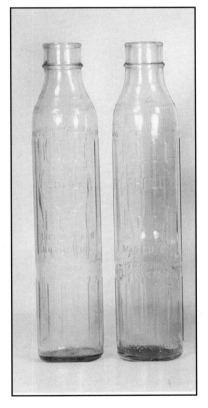

Shell Motor Oil *bottles*
Shell Oil Company
Houston, Texas
1 quart glass oil bottles 14½" tall with embossed lettering
$130.00 (C)

Shell Motor Oil *bottle storage case*
Shell Oil Company
Houston, Texas
14¾" x 15" x 11⅝" metal with hinged lid
(stamped with shell logo) case
included are 16 clear glass shell embossed lettering bottles
$400.00–$800.00 (C)

Simoniz Kleener
(art of man polishing early car & Simoniz crest)
half gallon tin, 5½" x 6"
$15.00 (B)

Sinclair Opaline Motor Oil *tin*
(dinosaur at bottom) mellowed 80 million years
Sinclair Refining Company
Chicago, Illinois
5 quart tin, 6½" diameter x 9½" tall
$50.00 (D)

Opaline Motor Oil *tin (old car art in center)*
Sinclair Refining Company
Chicago, Illinois
(Sinclair used the logo in the center of the
car radiator from 1916 until 1920.)
1 gallon tin, 11½" tall
$475.00 (B)

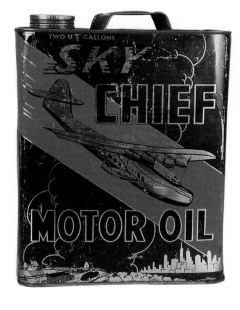

Sky Chief Motor Oil *tin (city and county scene at bottom)*
2 gallon tin, 11½" tall
$275.00 (B)

Pioneer Oil tin (covered wagon scene in center)
The Slimp Oil Company
San Antonio, Texas
1 gallon tin, 11" tall
$45.00 (D)

White Eagle Grease tin (white eagle art on side)
Socony-Vacuum Oil Company, Inc.
(Socony bought White Eagle Oil of Kansas City, Missouri, in 1930.
In 1931 Socony merged with Vacuum. Notice "White Eagle Division of
Socony-Vacuum Oil Co." on bottom of can.)
10 lb tin, 7¼" diameter x 9" tall
$50.00 (B)

Mobilgrease No. 4
Socony-Vacuum Oil Company, Inc.
100 pound tin
$35.00–$55.00 (C)

Courtesy of Gene Sonnen

Courtesy of Gene Sonnen

Mobilube
Socony-Vacuum Oil Company, Inc.
100 pound tin
$35.00–$55.00 (C)

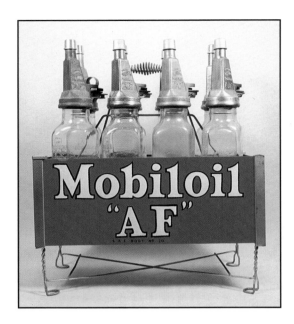

Mobiloil "AF"
Socony-Vacuum Oil Company, Inc.
8-quart glass bottles and wire rack with
restored sides and new caps on bottles
$675.00–$900.00 (C)

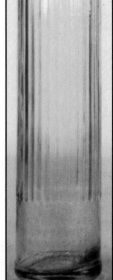

Socony *oil bottle*
Socony-Vacuum Oil Company, Inc.
1-quart glass bottle with metal pouring spout
15½" tall with embossed lettering
$75.00 (B)

Socony Globe Paraffine Candles *box*
Socony-Vacuum Oil Company, Inc.
wooden box with hinged lid, 15" x 12" x 12"
$50.00 (B)

Socony Motor Oil tin (logo in center)
(Standard Oil of New York used this style logo
in the center of the can from 1911 to 1931.)
Standard Oil Company of New York
26 Broadway; New York, New York
1 gallon tin, 11" tall
$50.00 (B)

Socony Kerosene Oil tin (logo in center)
(Standard Oil of New York also used
this style logo from 1911 to 1931.)
Standard Oil Company of New York
26 Broadway; New York, New York
1 gallon tin, 8" x 10"
$40.00 (B)

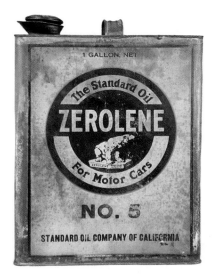

The Standard Oil Zerolene for Motor Cars tin
(polar bear in center)
Standard Oil Company of California
1 gallon tin, 8" x 11"
$35.00 (D)

4 glass oil bottles
(two are **Standard Polarine** & two are **Atlantic Refining**)
1-quart glass oil bottles with metal tops and lids
$220.00 for all four (B)

Sterling Motor Oil tin
(Sterling logo in center) 100% Pure Pennsylvania Oil
(Although Quaker State bought Sterling Oil in 1931, the Sterling Brand
was used into the 1960s. This can dates approximately 1923–1930.)
1 gallon tin, 7½" x 10"
$125.00 (D)

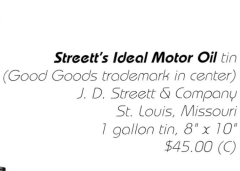

Streett's Ideal Motor Oil tin
(Good Goods trademark in center)
J. D. Streett & Company
St. Louis, Missouri
1 gallon tin, 8" x 10"
$45.00 (C)

Sturdy Motor Oil tin (single tree art in center)
2 gallon tin, 10½" tall
circa 1925–1945
$25.00 (B)

Sunoco steering gear lubricant tin (logo at top)
Sun Oil Company
Philadelphia, Pennsylvania
5 lb. tin, 6½" diameter x 5¼" tall
$30.00 (B)

Sunoco 8-quart bottle rack
Sun Oil Company
Philadelphia, Pennsylvania
14½" tall, 8 embossed glass bottles with new caps/all
Sunoco but not a matching set, and wire rack
$450.00 (B)

Finest Grease tin (featuring old car art)
Sun Oil Company
Philadelphia, Pennsylvania, U. S. A.
tin pail with handle, 6" diameter x 6" tall
$60.00 (B)

Super Penn Motor Oil tin
(highest quality red eagle in center)
Super Service Oil Company
New York, New York
2 gallon tin, 11" tall
$30.00 (B)

100% Pure Pennsylvania Motor Oil tin
(map in center depicting oil region)
Superior-Penn
Superior Oil Works
Warren, Pennsylvania
2 gallon tin, 10½" tall
$45.00 (B)

Texaco Motor Oil tin (Texaco logo in center)
The Texas Company
Port Arthur, Texas U.S.A.
(This was the first oil company to
have stations in all 50 states.)
1 gallon tin, 5" x 11"
$200.00 (B)

Texaco Motor Oil Heavy tin
(texaco logo in center)
The Texas Company
Port Arthur, Texas U.S.A.
half gallon easy grip tin, 6½" tall
$95.00 (B)

Texaco Motor Oil tin
(Texaco logo in center)
The Texas Company
Port Arthur, Texas U.S.A.
one gallon tin, 8½" x 5½"
$310.00 (B)

Texaco Marine Motor Oil tin
(art depicting boats in water at bottom)
(Notice the black edge around the green "T" in the center logo. This was used from 1936 into the 1940s when a white outline was adopted.)
The Texas Company
Port Arthur, Texas U.S.A.
1 gallon square tin, 9½" tall
$250.00 (B)

Texaco Aircraft Engine Oil tin made in USA
(green winged logo at bottom)
The Texas Company
Port Arthur, Texas U.S.A.
1 quart tin, 4" diameter x 5½" tall
$40.00 (B)

Texaco Aircraft Engine Oil tin
(Texaco logo in center)
The Texas Company
Port Arthur, Texas U.S.A.
1 quart tin, 4" x 5½"
$25.00 (B)

Texaco Home Lubricant tin
(Texaco logo at top with scene of houses)
The Texas Company
Port Arthur, Texas U.S.A.
3 oz. tin, 1¾" diameter x 6½" tall
$65.00 (D)

Texaco Outboard Motor Oil tin
(picture of outboard motor in center)
The Texas Company
Port Arthur, Texas U.S.A.
1 quart tin, 4" diameter x 5½" tall
$40.00 (D)

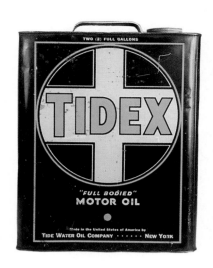

Tidex full bodied Motor Oil tin
Tide Water Oil Company
New York, New York
(This company was founded in 1887 and marketed the "Veedol" brand oil. In 1966 Tide Water
changed its name to Getty Oil.)
2 gallon tin, 8½" x 10½"
$75.00 (B)

Tiopet 100% pure Pennsylvania Motor Oil tin
(art work of Indian in full headdress at top)
Tiopet Motor Oil Company
1 quart tin, 4" diameter x 5½" tall
circa 1935–1945
$400.00 (B)

Take a spin with **Red Top Motor Oil** tin
(spinning red top in center and
scene with car in background)
Topp Oil & Supply Company
370 East Water Street
Milwaukee, Wisconsin
1 gallon tin, 8½" tall
$415.00 (B)

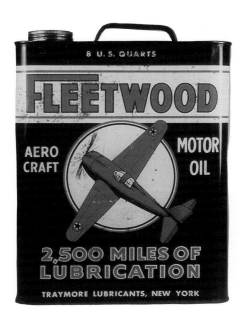

Fleetwood Aero-Craft Motor Oil *tin, 2,500 miles of lubrication (picture of red airplane in center)*
Traymore Lubricants
New York, New York
8 quart tin, 11" tall
$100.00 (D)

Royalene Motor Oil
(art of derrick, train car and early tank truck)
Traymore Lubricants
New York, New York
2 gallon tin
$110.00 (B)

Universal **Bonded Motor Oil** *tin*
(Universal trademark globe in center)
The Universal Motor Oils Co.
Wichita, Kansas
5 quart tin, 6½" diameter x 9½" tall
$140.00 (B)

The Universal Motor Oils Co. of Texas
Aeroil Motor Oil tin, 35¢ per qt., new dewaxed
(globe in center)
1 quart tin, 4" diameter x 5½" tall
$75.00 (B)

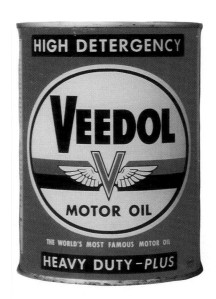

Veedol Motor Oil tin (red winged V in center of can)
Tide Water Oil Company
New York, New York
1 quart tin, 4" diameter x 5½" tall
$55.00 (B)

Long Life Motor Oil tin
(airplane and clouds in center of can)
Victor Oil Company
Detroit, Michigan
2 gallon tin, 5½" tall
circa 1935–1945
$85.00 (B)

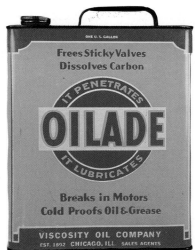

Oilade tin, Breaks in Motors, Cold Proofs Oil & Grease
Viscosity Oil Company
Chicago, Illinois
established 1892
1 gallon tin, 8" x 11"
$10.00 (B)

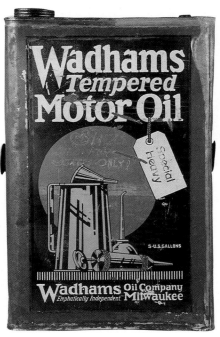

Wadhams Tempered Motor Oil tin
(picture of oil cans and grease gun at bottom)
Wadhams Oil Company
Milwaukee, Wisconsin
Emphatically Independent, established 1879
(Wadhams Oil Company was purchased by Vacuum
Oil Company in 1930, and they then merged in
1931 with Socony to form Socony-Vacuum Oil.)
5 gallon tin
$25.00 (D)

Wadhams Tempered Motor Oil *tin*
(picture of oil cans and grease gun at top)
Emphatically Independent, established 1879
Wadhams Oil Company
Milwaukee, Wisconsin
5 gallon easy pour tin, 14½" diameter x 16¾" tall
$195.00 (D)

High Grade Cup Grease *tin*
(Phillips products symbol at top)
Waite Phillips Company
Tulsa, Oklahoma
(Belame Independent Oil & Gas Co. of Tulsa was eventually
purchased by Phillips Petroleum of Bartlesville, Oklahoma.)
10 lb tin, 7½" diameter x 7¼" tall
$45.00 (B)

Oneida Motor Oil *tin*
(art of Indian with blanket in center)
West Penn Oil Company, Inc.
Warren, Pennsylvania
1 quart tin, 4" diameter x 5½" tall
$100.00 (B)

Oilzum Fabric Cleaner *tin*
(art of Oilzum Man in center)
White & Bagley Company
Worcester, Massachusetts U. S. A.
1 pint tin, 3" x 5¾"
$145.00 (B)

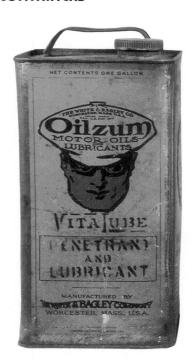

Oilzum Vita Lube tin (art of Oilzum Man at top center)
White & Bagley Company
Worcester, Massachusetts U. S. A.
(Oilzum products collectibles always seem to bring a high price.
Beware of reproductions especially in the sign category.)
1 gallon tin, 5" x 9½"
$145.00 (D)

Oilzum tin
(art of Oilzum Man in the O of Oilzum)
White & Bagley Company
Worcester, Massachusetts U. S. A.
5 lb. tin, 5¾" diameter x 7½" tall
$75.00 (B)

Star Zero-Flo Motor Oil tin
(art of car at bottom)
Whiting Oil Company
2 gallon tin, 8½" x 10½"
$75.00 (B)

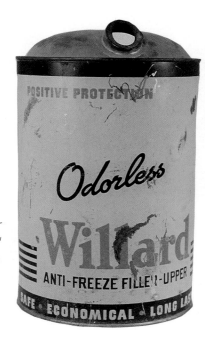

Odorless Willard Anti-freeze filler-upper
tin with handle and spout, 7" x 9¼"
$100.00 (B*)

Empire Motor Oil tin/Quality since 1879
Wolf's Head Oil Refining Company Inc.
Oil City, Pennsylvania
5 gallon tin, 16" tall
$35.00 (B)

Wonder-Mist Cleaner Polisher *tin*
(ligthograph of man cleaning early car in center)
(back has lithograph of woman cleaning table)
The Wonder-Mist Company/Manufacturers
Boston-Chicago-New York
half gallon tin, 5" x 8"
$130.00 (B)

Ronson Motor Oil *tin*
(scene with car, boat, and airplane in center)
Wynne Oil Company
Philadelphia, Pennsylvania
$100.00 (B)

Zurnoil for Automobiles *tin*
O. F. Zurn Company
Philadelphia, Pennsylvania
1 gallon tin, 9¼" x 8¾"
$55.00 (D)

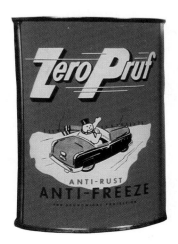

Zero Pruf Anti-rust Anti-Freeze *tin*
(art of snowman driving car in snow scene)
1 quart tin, 4" x 5½"
$95.00 (B)

This chapter is a mixture of items that wouldn't fit anywhere else. For most collectors this chapter will hold the "fill in" items. For others their main collecting focus might be on these pages. While I might like the glow of gas globes in my office, additional pieces such as maps or displays will make an attractive addition to the globes. These add on items seem to help complete most collections.

You might find some of these items that for years went overlooked are now coming into their own market place. For example, maps with good graphics that just a few years ago could be bought for a song are commanding fair market prices.

Whatever your method of madness is in collecting, hopefully this chapter will help.

Courtesy of Gene Sonnen

Ace High Thermometer
Midwest Oil Company
red, white & blue porcelain thermometer
(See Wil-Flo sign in the sign chapter)
$1,700.00–$1,900.00 (C) (#821)
(note: All Ace High collectibles
command a very high market value.)

Amalie Motor Oil Thermometer
*9" diameter glass front,
Centigrade/Fahrenheit thermometer
$85.00 (D)*

Amalie Motor Oil Clock
(with art of oil cans at 12, 3, 6 & 9)
15" diameter glass front, clock
$250.00 (D)

Astrostar Tires
(art of jet at center top) tire rack
13" x 9" painted tin tire rack
$45.00 (B)

Atlantic flying A *map rack*
8½" x 36" black, white and red metal rack
$110.00 (B)

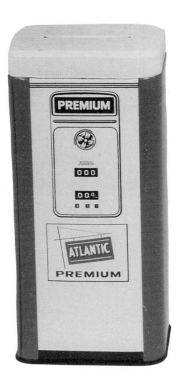

Atlantic *premium pump bank*
5" tall, blue, white, and red tin bank
$65.00 (D)

Atlas battery bank
3" tall, black and red metal bank
$25.00–$30.00 (C)

Auto Lite Spark Plug Cabinet
13" x 18½" painted metal with glass front cabinet
hinged door on back for hidden storage
$95.00 (D)

Automobile Lubrication booklet
Standard Oil of Indiana
Chicago, Illinois
cooling, lubrication, and troubleshooting booklet
$35.00 (D)

Blue Crown Spark Plug Display
14" x 16½" blue, white & gray tin display
$190.00 (B)

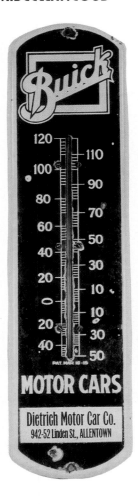

Buick Counter Display
(picture of 1960 Buick)
19⅝" x 15¾" wood frame, glass faced
light-up display
circa 1960
$65.00 (D)

Buick Motor Cars Thermometer
Dietrich Motor Car Company
942-52 Linden Street, Allentown; circa 1915
7¼" x 27" porcelain thermometer
patented March 16-15
$325.00 (C)

Cadillac Service Clock
(Cadillac logo in center)
round yellow plastic, glass lens clock
$175.00 (C)

Calso Gasoline Road Map Rack
12½" x 20" 3 painted metal shelves map rack
$95.00 (B)

Champion Spark Plug Radio
14" tall red, white, gray & black radio
$75.00 (D)

Chevrolet Dealer Used Car Committee 1937 Cigar Box
(Chevy Logo embossed on lid within art of diamond)
12" x 2½" x 9¼" wood ornate cigar box
circa 1937 (scarce)
$250.00 (B)

Courtesy of Gene Sonnen

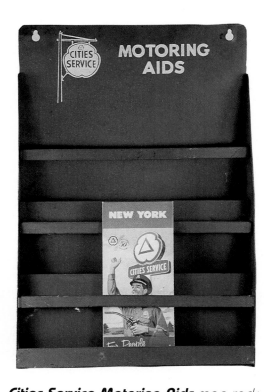

Cities Service *toy wrecker truck*
$275.00–$325.00 (C)

Cities Service Motoring Aids *map rack*
(Cities Service logo at top left)
13" x 19" painted metal rack
$95.00 (B)

Conoco Hottest Brand Going Lighter
*(art of cowboy with branding iron
of Conoco logo)
Continental Oil Company
2" x 1¾" lighter
$30.00 (D)*

Cranepenn Motor Oil
*L. M. Crane & Co.
Established 1860
Boston, Massachusetts
3½" diameter pocket mirror & paperweight
$75.00 (D)*

D-X *license plate reflector
Dura-Products Mfg. Company
Canton, Ohio
5½" x 4" metal reflector
$25.00 (D)*

D-X *pump glass
13" x 5⅜" painted glass pump panel
$30.00–$45.00 (C)*

Du Pont Denatured Alcohol Anti-Rust Anti-Freeze *thermometer*
8" x 38⅜" painted metal
$95.00 (C)

Erie Art Deco *cast iron air dispenser*
circa 1930s
$1,550.00–$1,850.00 (C)

Courtesy of Glen Thompson

Esso Salt & Pepper
1" x 2¾" x ¾" plastic shakers
$25.00 (D)

Esso Lubrication Chart 1940
(contains lubrication details on vehicles
rom 1940 and previous five years)
10½" x 15½" spiral bound chart
$15.00 (D)

Esso paint stencil
stencil for heating oil for 55 gallon drums
$75.00 (D)

Ethyl convention hat
circa 1930s
cloth hat
$30.00 (D)

Exide *battery display rack*
23½" x 46½" metal (with tin sign at top) rack
circa 1940
$125.00 (D)

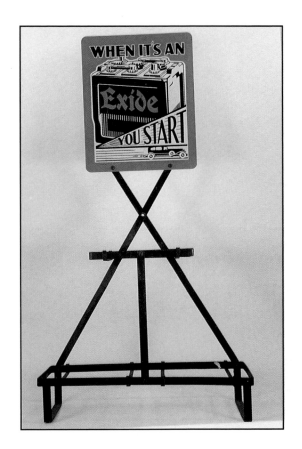

Exide *battery display rack*
40" tall metal & tin rack
$185.00–$200.00 (C)

Firestone Tires Clock
15¼" square wood frame with glass front clock
$200.00 (C)

Firestone Tires *ashtray*
5¾" diameter x 1½" deep rubber and glass ashtray
$35.00 (D)

Fisk Tire Rack *(Fisk logo top center)*
metal tire holder rack
$125.00 (B)

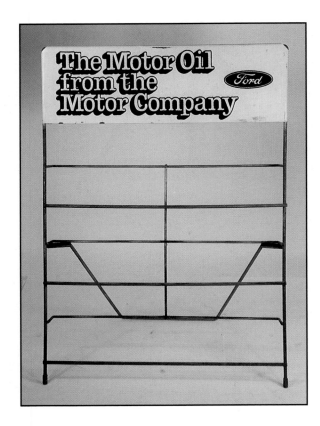

Courtesy of Gene Sonnen

Ford Motor Company *oil display rack*
18" x 25" metal oil rack
$65.00 (B)

Original Ford Motor Company Sales & Service *clock*
(beware of reproductions of this style of clock)
metal frame and glass clock
$600.00–$700.00 (C)

Golden Tip Plate
Golden Tip Gasoline Company
Louisville, Kentucky
Taylor, Smith & Taylor Pottery Company
$55.00–$90.00 (C)

Viscoyl Notebook
Golden Tip Gasoline
The Stoll Oil Refining Company Inc.
Louisville, Kentucky
1939, 1949, 1950 notebooks with car care
facts plus short stories with a moral
$12.00–$25.00 (C)

Gulf Gas Measuring Stick (used to check gas levels before the advent of gas gauges)
Gulf Refining Company Inc.
$15.00–$20.00 (C)

Gulf Funny Weekly
published weekly and free for Gulf Stations
art by Stan Schendel
Gulf Refining Company Inc.
$55.00 (C)

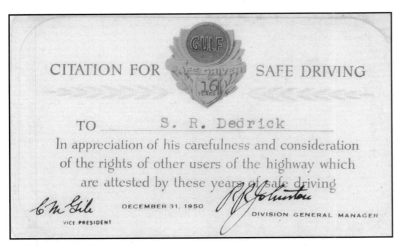

CITATION FOR SAFE DRIVING

TO _____ S. R. Dedrick _____

In appreciation of his carefulness and consideration
of the rights of other users of the highway which
are attested by these years of safe driving

C M Gile
VICE PRESIDENT

DECEMBER 31, 1950

R R Johnston
DIVISION GENERAL MANAGER

Courtesy of Frances Nicholson

Gulf Safe Driving Citation
*issued to S. R. Dedrick for 16 years safe
driving for the Gulf Refining Company Inc.
December 31, 1950*
$15.00 (C)

Gulf *Tour Guide Service Map Rack*
9⅛" x 18" metal rack
$75.00 (C)

Gulf *sprayer & Penetrating Oil can tin containers*
$40.00 (for both) (B)

Gulf Oil Lubricants *Display*
10" x 12" x 4½" metal display
$250.00 (D)

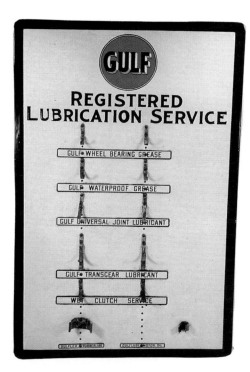

Gulf Registered Lubrication Service *rack*
Gulf logo at top
$150.00 (B)

Gulf Oil *rack*
25½" tall wire frame (tin 2-sided sign at top)
$75.00 (D)

Gulf *gas price sign with attachment arm*
Gulf logo at top
$225.00–$275.00 (C)

Hastings Oil Filters Display
16" tall display with Hastings man art
$55.00 (B)

Hood Tube Tire box
5"x15"x 5" cardboard box
(fairly rare)
$185.00 (B)

Island Pump Lights (pair)
fluorescent tubes under heavy glass
cylinders with dimensional lighting on
top all glass is in good condition
$350.00–$450.00 (C)

Kendall 2000 mile oil display rack with cans
13" x 39½" x 13" metal rack with sign at top
$425.00 (B)

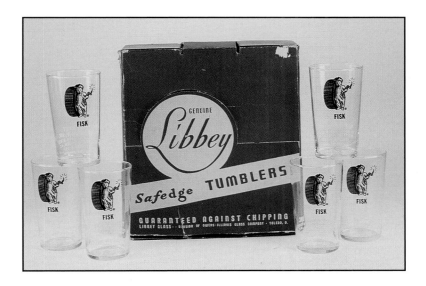

Libbey Safedge *Tumblers*
featuring Fisk Tires logo
6 glasses with box
(glass is 2½" diameter x 4⅝" tall)
Piedmont Tire Service Inc.
121 South Main Street
Winston-Salem, North Carolina
Phone: 5-2421/Modern Recapping
$65.00 (D)

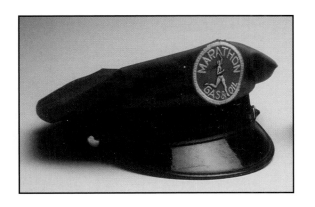

Marathon *Winter Uniform Hat*
Marathon runner on patch
$95.00–$150.00 (C)

Mac Bulldog *ashtray*
4½" tall silver ashtray
design patent 87931
$25.00 (B)

Marathon Travel Bureau Service *Map Rack*
$200.00–$250.00 (C)

Courtesy of Gene Sonnen

Marx *toy pumps*
9½" x 6" tin with milk glass globes,
battery operated early pumps
$275.00 (B)

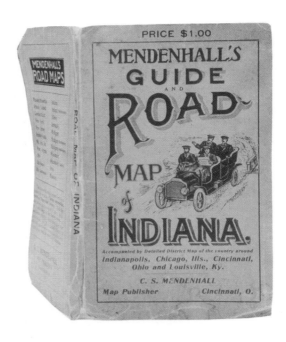

Michelin Ashtray with Michelin Man
6" diameter x 4¾" tall molded plastic ashtray
circa 1940's
$75.00 (B)

Mendenhall's Guide and Road Map of Indiana
Copyright 1906/price $1.00
4½" x 7¼" folded paper map
descriptions inside include whether road
is level, hilly, gravel, dirt or some dirt
$25.00–$50.00 (C)

Michelin *stained glass*
33½" x 31¼" leaded stained glass in wood frame
$900.00 (B)

Micro-Lube *wire display rack*
20" x 34" metal rack with metal sign at top
$75.00 (B)

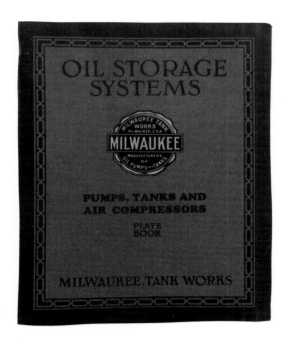

Milwaukee Oil Storage Systems *Book*
Milwaukee Tank Works
book contains pumps, tanks,
and air compressors
8¼" x 10" paper bound book
printed in USA 5/2/24
$55.00–$75.00 (C)

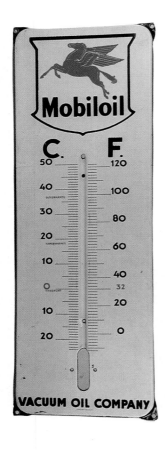

Mobiloil *porcelain thermometer*
Vacuum Oil Company
8" x 23" with Pegasus shield on top
$250.00 (B)

Mobiloil *hat (correct buttons)*
summer uniform hat
$100.00–$200.00 (C)

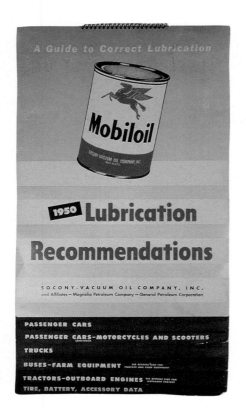

Mobiloil Lubrication Recommendations
circa 1950
Socony Vacuum Oil Company and Affiliates: Magnolia Petroleum Co.–General Petroleum Corporation
16" x 28" paper guide to correct lubrication
$75.00 (B)

Mobiloil *Calendar*
Follow the Magnolia Trail
Through the Scenic Wonderland
of the Southwest
14" x 23", 1933 paper calendar
$95.00 (C)

Mobil Service *Clock with Pegasus at center*
Metal frame with glass lens
$195.00 (D)

Mobilgas Friendly Service *Thermometer*
4½" x 34¾" porcelain
circa 1920 – 1930
$265.00 (D)

Courtesy of Gene Sonnen

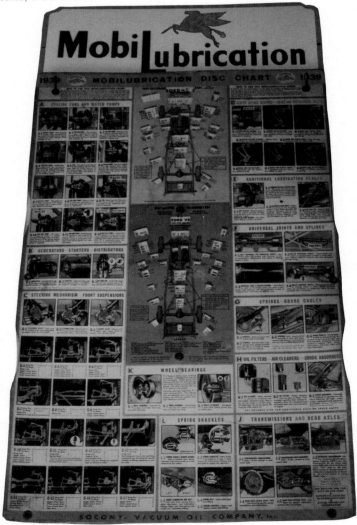

MobiLubrication *chart*
porcelain chart with service wheels on side to dial in your vehicle
circa 1939
$200.00–$300.00 (C)

Courtesy of Gene Sonnen

Large Pegasus
referred to by collectors as the
"cookie cutter" model
$950.00–$1,100.00 each (C)
(Note: These are left and right facing
models. When buying a unit in parts,
make sure all parts are for either
right or left model.)

Mobil *window spray bottle*
Socony-Vacuum Oil Company
glass bottle with paper label
$25.00–$50.00 (C)

Mobiloil 1938 Calendar
follow the Magnolia Trail through the Southwest
paper calendar
$100.00–$125.00 (C)

Mohawk Tires Display Rack
13" x 9" painted tin rack
$75.00 (D)

Toy cast iron gas pump
no company name
6½" tall, red with black rubber hose
crank on back turns dial on front
$400.00 (B)

Mobiloil Pegasus
3' porcelain cut-out Pegasus
$575.00 (D)

Inflate your tires here air dispenser
no company name
49" tall cast iron air dispenser with embossed lettering
The Air Scale Company
Toledo, Ohio USA
$850.00–$1,000.00 (C)

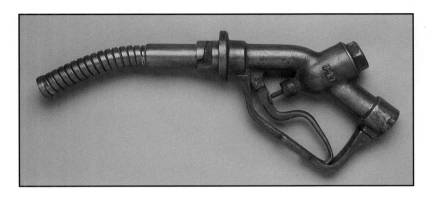

pump nozzle
no company name
17" tall brass gas pump hose nozzle U17
$20.00–$55.00 (C)

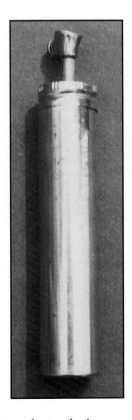

shirt pocket window spritzer
no company name
$50.00–$75.00 (C)

Oilzum Motor Oil *Clock (Oilzum man at center)*
16" square plastic with metal back clock
$175.00 (D)

Genuine Packard Cable box
The Packard Electric Company
4½" x 4" x 4" metal edged cardboard box
$10.00 (D)

Oilzum Motor Oil Clock (Oilzum man at center)
14½" diameter glass lens clock
$950.00 (B)

Double Game Board Lincoln Highway and Checkers
(art of family traveling in early car with mountains in background on lid)
Parker Brothers Inc.
$90.00 (C)

Packard Automotive Cable display rack
The Packard Electric Company
10" x 36" painted tin display
$35.00 (B)

Pennzoil Thermometer
glass faced with Liberty Bell in center
$200.00 (B)

Phillips 66 silver anniversary
paperweight mirror
circa 1955
3½" diameter
$120.00 (B)

Premium & Regular *pump glasses*
10¾" x 3½" glass inserts
$25.00 (C)

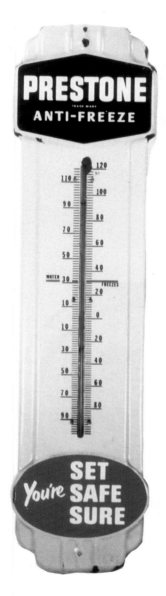

Quaker State Motor Oil *Clock*
$350.00–$500.00 (C)

Red Crown Gasoline Ethyl *pamphlet*
extolling the virtues of Ethyl Gasoline. One
suggestion is that it is important to drain
your gas tank before filling it with Ethyl
Gasoline! Standard Oil Company of Indiana
$10.00 (C)

Prestone Anti-Freeze *thermometer*
8¾" x 36" porcelain
circa 1940s
$225.00 (D)

Red Seal Dry Battery Thermometer
Beech Cosoctin, O
dated March 16, 1915
7¼" x 26¾" porcelain
$175.00 (C)

Satin Oil cast iron lollipop sign base
Satin Oil Corporation
Tulsa, Oklahoma
$45.00–$75.00 (C)

Schrader Tire Gauge Can
6" diameter x 14¾" tall can
circa 1920–1930
$160.00 (B)

Approved Shell Service hat pin
rare cloisonne pin
with space for name tag
$300.00–$400.00 (C)

Tootsietoy Shell tanker truck
6" x 1¾" pressed steel toy
$75.00 (C)

Shell road map of Michigan
1933 paper map
containing Shell transcontinental mileage chart.
Legend records dirt to paved roads.
$30.00 (D)

Sinclair Dino
Vinyl inflatable dinosaur figure
$25.00 (C)

Sinclair Oil Wagon
restored
$5,500.00 (C)

Sinclair Map of Michigan
art of older car with couple in front
of Sinclair Station
$35.00 (D)

Courtesy of Gene Sonnen

**Red Crown Gasoline/Standard Oil
Company/Polarine Oil** box
wooden box from late 1800s
horse-drawn wagon
$500.00–$700.00 (C)

Red Crown Gasoline/Standard Oil Company
horse drawn gasoline tanker
manufactured in 1895 in Mason City, Iowa
restored by Gene Sonnen
$6,000.00–$7,000.00 (C)

Courtesy of Gene Sonnen

Standard Oil *research test car bracket with crown in center of wings*
$45.00–$75.00 (C)

Standard Oil Company Incorporated in Kentucky *Engraving Plate*
$175.00 (C)

Courtesy of John & Vicki Mahan

Standard Oil Company

Joe Darnall/Agent
LA 7-4391
Benton, Kentucky
3¼" x 11½" metal thermometer
$95.00 (C)

Standard Oil *calendar top*
with artwork of man at pump
Standard Oil Company of New York
Socony Gasoline and Motor Oil
$90.00(B)

Standard Oil *summer uniform hat*
$150.00–$200.00(C)

Standard Oil *metal lubster lid*
Standard Oil Company of Indiana
7⅛" diameter cast metal lid
$25.00–$35.00(C)
(Beware of repos.)

Studebaker Batteries *Clock*
(logo at top center)
15¼" square metal framed glass front clock
$150.00 (C)

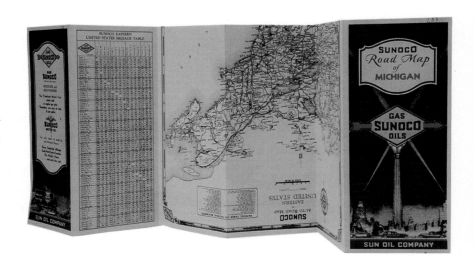

Sunoco *road map of Michigan*
art of older model car driving under
the Sunoco diamond logo
(legend records dirt to paved roads)
$15.00–$18.00 (C)

Texaco 1936 calendar
The Texas Company
Port Arthur, Texas
spiral bound calendar featuring different
art with each month
$145.00 (C)

Texaco gas mileage finder
Bud Husing Texaco
Rockport, Missouri
$10.00 (C)

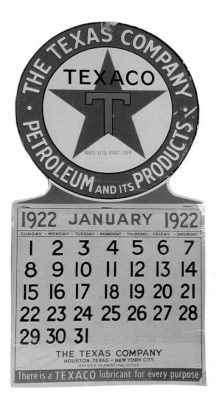

Texaco thermometer
Roy E. Gourley
Lebanon, Missouri
12" diameter glass faced thermometer
$500.00 (B)

Texaco 1922 calendar
The Texas Company
Houston, Texas/New York City
13" x 25" die-cut cardboard calendar
$185.00 (B)

Texaco toy tanker ship with box
(dealer offer)
26½" x 5" motorized plastic toy with
Texaco logo on smoke stacks
$200.00 (C)

Texaco toy fire chief hat
8" high plastic fireman's hat with logo in center
$75.00 (D)

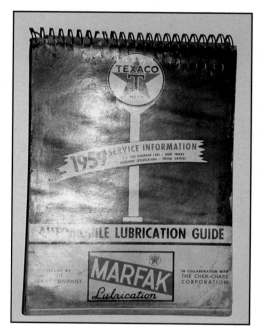

Texaco 1959 service information guide
spiral bound cardboard and paper
$35.00–$40.00 (C)

Texaco touring service map holder
painted metal holder with maps
$110.00 (B)

Tide Water Flying A credit card machine
Farrington Manufacturing Company
Needham Heights, Massachusetts
14" x 6¼" x 11½" metal machine
$75.00 (B)

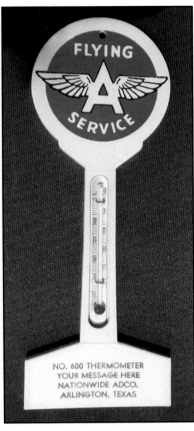

Tydol Flying A *thermometer*
2½" x 7" plastic thermometer
$55.00 (C)

Courtesy of John and Vicki Mahan

Tiolene Motor Oil *Lubrication Chart*
Pure Oil Company
linen lube chart
this chart lists all makes of vehicles for 1931
$75.00–$100.00 (C)

Tokheim *display cabinet*
model 98A
restored metal cabinet
$1,800.00–$2,200.00 (C)

Courtesy of Larry & Krissy Wingate

Courtesy of Larry & Krissy Wingate

Tokheim display cabinet
model 98A
restored metal cabinet
$1,800.00–$2,200.00 (C)

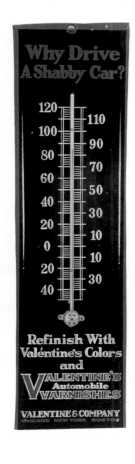

United Gasoline Super Charged
glass ashtray
$5.00–$10.00 (C)

Valentine's Varnishes thermometer
Valentine & Company
Chicago, New York, Boston
5½" x 20" celluloid thermometer
$145.00 (C)

Vanderbilt Premium Tires Clock
Pam Clock Company Inc.
New Rochelle, New York
circa 1958
14½" diameter, metal frame with glass face
$165.00 (C)

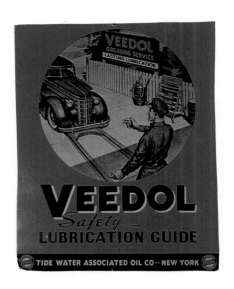
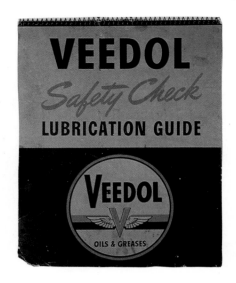

Veedol Lubrication Guides
Tide Water Associated Oil Co. New York
13½" x 17½"
$50.00–$60.00 (for both) (C)

Wolf's Head Motor Oil Light
14" x 13½" x 5" cardboard body light
$10.00 (B)

Whiz Patch Outfit display
14½" x 21¼" painted metal
display rack
$300.00 (B)

Wolf's Head Motor Oil & Lubes round clock
$375.00 (C)

Pictured above is an early, probably 1920s, White Eagle station.
Note eagle globes and cast iron eagle in front of drive.
Center globe is a very rare White Eagle 3-piece glass globe.

X-Powder *counter display*
11" x 15" cardboard display with tins
$150.00–$200.00 (C)

White Eagle
cast iron drive statue
$750.00–$1,000.00 (C)

INDEX

GLOBES
(Pages 13–75)

PUMPS

(Pages 79-132)

SIGNS

(Pages 134–232)

CONTAINERS
(Pages 236–279)

MISCELLANEOUS

(Pages 280–319)

COLLECTOR BOOKS

I n f o r m i n g   T o d a y ' s   C o l l e c t o r

For over two decades we have been keeping collectors informed on trends and values in all fields of antiques and collectibles.

COLLECTOR BOOKS
Informing Today's Collector

5035	Standard Encyclopedia of **Carnival Glass**, 6th Ed., Edwards/Carwile	$24.95
5036	Standard **Carnival Glass** Price Guide, 11th Ed., Edwards/Carwile	$9.95
5272	Standard Encyclopedia of **Opalescent Glass**, 3rd ed., Edwards	$24.95
4731	**Stemware Identification**, Featuring Cordials with Values, Florence	$24.95
3326	**Very Rare Glassware** of the Depression Years, 3rd Series, Florence	$24.95
4732	**Very Rare Glassware** of the Depression Years, 5th Series, Florence	$24.95
4656	**Westmoreland Glass**, Wilson	$24.95

POTTERY

4927	**ABC Plates & Mugs**, Lindsay	$24.95
4929	**American Art Pottery**, Sigafoose	$24.95
4630	**American Limoges**, Limoges	$24.95
1312	**Blue & White Stoneware**, McNerney	$9.95
1958	So. Potteries **Blue Ridge Dinnerware**, 3rd Ed., Newbound	$14.95
1959	**Blue Willow**, 2nd Ed., Gaston	$14.95
4848	Ceramic **Coin Banks**, Stoddard	$19.95
4851	Collectible **Cups & Saucers**, Harran	$18.95
4709	Collectible **Kay Finch**, Biography, Identification & Values, Martinez/Frick	$18.95
1373	Collector's Encyclopedia of **American Dinnerware**, Cunningham	$24.95
4931	Collector's Encyclopedia of **Bauer Pottery**, Chipman	$24.95
4932	Collector's Encyclopedia of **Blue Ridge Dinnerware**, Vol. II, Newbound	$24.95
4658	Collector's Encyclopedia of **Brush-McCoy Pottery**, Huxford	$24.95
5034	Collector's Encyclopedia of **California Pottery**, 2nd Ed., Chipman	$24.95
2133	Collector's Encyclopedia of **Cookie Jars**, Roerig	$24.95
3723	Collector's Encyclopedia of **Cookie Jars**, Book II, Roerig	$24.95
4939	Collector's Encyclopedia of **Cookie Jars**, Book III, Roerig	$24.95
4638	Collector's Encyclopedia of **Dakota Potteries**, Dommel	$24.95
5040	Collector's Encyclopedia of **Fiesta**, 8th Ed., Huxford	$19.95
4718	Collector's Encyclopedia of **Figural Planters & Vases**, Newbound	$19.95
3961	Collector's Encyclopedia of **Early Noritake**, Alden	$24.95
1439	Collector's Encyclopedia of **Flow Blue China**, Gaston	$19.95
3812	Collector's Encyclopedia of **Flow Blue China**, 2nd Ed., Gaston	$24.95
3813	Collector's Encyclopedia of **Hall China**, 2nd Ed., Whitmyer	$24.95
3431	Collector's Encyclopedia of **Homer Laughlin China**, Jasper	$24.95
1276	Collector's Encyclopedia of **Hull Pottery**, Roberts	$19.95
3962	Collector's Encyclopedia of **Lefton China**, DeLozier	$19.95
4855	Collector's Encyclopedia of **Lefton China**, Book II, DeLozier	$19.95
2210	Collector's Encyclopedia of **Limoges Porcelain**, 2nd Ed., Gaston	$24.95
2334	Collector's Encyclopedia of **Majolica Pottery**, Katz-Marks	$19.95
1358	Collector's Encyclopedia of **McCoy Pottery**, Huxford	$19.95
3963	Collector's Encyclopedia of **Metlox Potteries**, Gibbs Jr.	$24.95
3837	Collector's Encyclopedia of **Nippon Porcelain**, Van Patten	$24.95
2089	Collector's Ency. of **Nippon Porcelain**, 2nd Series, Van Patten	$24.95
1665	Collector's Ency. of **Nippon Porcelain**, 3rd Series, Van Patten	$24.95
4712	Collector's Ency. of **Nippon Porcelain**, 4th Series, Van Patten	$24.95
1447	Collector's Encyclopedia of **Noritake**, Van Patten	$19.95
1037	Collector's Encyclopedia of **Occupied Japan**, 1st Series, Florence	$14.95
1038	Collector's Encyclopedia of **Occupied Japan**, 2nd Series, Florence	$14.95
2088	Collector's Encyclopedia of **Occupied Japan**, 3rd Series, Florence	$14.95
2019	Collector's Encyclopedia of **Occupied Japan**, 4th Series, Florence	$14.95
2335	Collector's Encyclopedia of **Occupied Japan**, 5th Series, Florence	$14.95
4951	Collector's Encyclopedia of **Old Ivory China**, Hillman	$24.95
3964	Collector's Encyclopedia of **Pickard China**, Reed	$24.95
3877	Collector's Encyclopedia of **R.S. Prussia**, 4th Series, Gaston	$24.95
1034	Collector's Encyclopedia of **Roseville Pottery**, Huxford	$19.95
1035	Collector's Encyclopedia of **Roseville Pottery**, 2nd Ed., Huxford	$19.95
4856	Collector's Encyclopedia of **Russel Wright**, 2nd Ed., Kerr	$24.95
4713	Collector's Encyclopedia of **Salt Glaze Stoneware**, Taylor/Lowrance	$24.95
3314	Collector's Encyclopedia of **Van Briggle** Art Pottery, Sasicki	$24.95
4563	Collector's Encyclopedia of **Wall Pockets**, Newbound	$19.95
2111	Collector's Encyclopedia of **Weller Pottery**, Huxford	$29.95
3876	Collector's Guide to **Lu-Ray Pastels**, Meehan	$18.95
3814	Collector's Guide to **Made in Japan** Ceramics, White	$18.95
4646	Collector's Guide to **Made in Japan** Ceramics, Book II, White	$18.95
2339	Collector's Guide to **Shawnee Pottery**, Vanderbilt	$19.95

1425	**Cookie Jars**, Westfall	$9.95
3440	**Cookie Jars**, Book II, Westfall	$19.95
4924	Figural & Novelty **Salt & Pepper Shakers**, 2nd Series, Davern	$24.95
2379	Lehner's Ency. of **U.S. Marks** on Pottery, Porcelain & China	$24.95
4722	**McCoy Pottery**, Collector's Reference & Value Guide, Hanson/Nissen	$19.95
4726	**Red Wing Art Pottery**, 1920s–1960s, Dollen	$19.95
1670	**Red Wing Collectibles**, DePasquale	$9.95
1440	**Red Wing Stoneware**, DePasquale	$9.95
1632	**Salt & Pepper Shakers**, Guarnaccia	$9.95
5091	**Salt & Pepper Shakers** II, Guarnaccia	$18.95
2220	**Salt & Pepper Shakers** III, Guarnaccia	$14.95
3443	**Salt & Pepper Shakers** IV, Guarnaccia	$18.95
3738	**Shawnee Pottery**, Mangus	$24.95
4629	Turn of the Century **American Dinnerware**, 1880s–1920s, Jasper	$24.95
3327	**Watt Pottery** – Identification & Value Guide, Morris	$19.95

OTHER COLLECTIBLES

4704	Antique & Collectible **Buttons**, Wisniewski	$19.95
2269	Antique **Brass & Copper** Collectibles, Gaston	$16.95
1880	Antique **Iron**, McNerney	$9.95
3872	Antique **Tins**, Dodge	$24.95
4845	Antique **Typewriters & Office Collectibles**, Rehr	$19.95
1714	**Black** Collectibles, Gibbs	$19.95
1128	**Bottle** Pricing Guide, 3rd Ed., Cleveland	$7.95
4636	**Celluloid Collectibles**, Dunn	$14.95
3718	Collectible **Aluminum**, Grist	$16.95
4560	Collectible **Cats**, An Identification & Value Guide, Book II, Fyke	$19.95
4852	Collectible **Compact Disc** Price Guide 2, Cooper	$17.95
2018	Collector's Encyclopedia of **Granite Ware**, Greguire	$24.95
3430	Collector's Encyclopedia of **Granite Ware**, Book 2, Greguire	$24.95
4705	Collector's Guide to **Antique Radios**, 4th Ed., Bunis	$18.95
3880	Collector's Guide to **Cigarette Lighters**, Flanagan	$17.95
4637	Collector's Guide to **Cigarette Lighters**, Book II, Flanagan	$17.95
4942	Collector's Guide to **Don Winton Designs**, Ellis	$19.95
3966	Collector's Guide to **Inkwells**, Identification & Values, Badders	$18.95
4947	Collector's Guide to **Inkwells**, Book II, Badders	$19.95
4948	Collector's Guide to **Letter Openers**, Grist	$19.95
4862	Collector's Guide to **Toasters** & Accessories, Greguire	$19.95
4652	Collector's Guide to **Transistor Radios**, 2nd Ed., Bunis	$16.95
4864	Collector's Guide to **Wallace Nutting Pictures**, Ivankovich	$18.95
1629	**Doorstops**, Identification & Values, Bertoia	$9.95
4567	Figural **Napkin Rings**, Gottschalk & Whitson	$9.95
4717	Figural **Nodders**, Includes Bobbin' Heads and Swayers, Irtz	$19.95
3968	**Fishing Lure** Collectibles, Murphy/Edmisten	$24.95
5259	**Flea Market Trader**, 12th Ed., Huxford	$9.95
4944	**Flue Covers**, Collector's Value Guide, Meckley	$12.95
4945	**G-Men and FBI Toys** and Collectibles, Whitworth	$18.95
5263	**Garage Sale & Flea Market Annual**, 7th Ed.	$19.95
3819	**General Store Collectibles**, Wilson	$24.95
5159	Huxford's Collectible **Advertising**, 4th Ed.	$24.95
2216	**Kitchen Antiques**, 1790–1940, McNerney	$14.95
4950	The **Lone Ranger**, Collector's Reference & Value Guide, Felbinger	$18.95
2026	**Railroad** Collectibles, 4th Ed., Baker	$14.95
5167	**Schroeder's Antiques** Price Guide, 17th Ed., Huxford	$12.95
5007	**Silverplated Flatware**, Revised 4th Edition, Hagan	$18.95
1922	Standard **Old Bottle** Price Guide, Sellari	$14.95
5154	Summers' Guide to **Coca-Cola**, 2nd Ed.	$19.95
4952	Summers' Pocket Guide to **Coca-Cola** Identifications	$9.95
3892	**Toy & Miniature Sewing Machines**, Thomas	$18.95
4876	**Toy & Miniature Sewing Machines**, Book II, Thomas	$24.95
5144	Value Guide to **Advertising Memorabilia**, 2nd Ed., Summers	$19.95
3977	Value Guide to **Gas Station** Memorabilia, Summers & Priddy	$24.95
4877	Vintage **Bar Ware**, Visakay	$24.95
4935	The W.F. Cody **Buffalo Bill** Collector's Guide with Values	$24.95
5281	**Wanted to Buy**, 7th Edition	$9.95

Schroeder's ANTIQUES Price Guide

Schroeder's ANTIQUES Price Guide

OUR #1 BEST-SELLER!

Identification & Values of Over 50,000 Antiques & Collectibles

8½ x 11, 608 Pages, $12.95

. . . is the #1 bestselling antiques & collectibles value guide on the market today, and here's why . . .

- *More than 450 advisors, well-known dealers, and top-notch collectors work together with our editors to bring you accurate information regarding pricing and identification.*

- *More than 45,000 items in almost 550 categories are listed along with hundreds of sharp original photos that illustrate not only the rare and unusual, but the common, popular collectibles as well.*

- *Each large close-up shot shows important details clearly. Every subject is represented with histories and background information, a feature not found in any of our competitors' publications.*

- *Our editors keep abreast of newly developing trends, often adding several new categories a year as the need arises.*

If it merits the interest of today's collector, you'll find it in *Schroeder's*. And you can feel confident that the information we publish is up to date and accurate. Our advisors thoroughly check each category to spot inconsistencies, listings that may not be entirely reflective of market dealings, and lines too vague to be of merit. Only the best of the lot remains for publication.

Without doubt, you'll find
SCHROEDER'S ANTIQUES PRICE GUIDE
the only one to buy for
reliable information and values.

COLLECTOR BOOKS
A Division of Schroeder Publishing Co., Inc.